BRIDGING THE RELATION GAP

Bridging the Relationship Gap

Connecting with Children Facing Adversity

SARA LANGWORTHY, PHD

Redleaf Press®
www.redleafpress.org
800-423-8309

Published by Redleaf Press
10 Yorkton Court
St. Paul, MN 55117
www.redleafpress.org

First edition 2015
Cover design by Jim Handrigan
Interior design by Wendy Holdman
Typeset in Arno Pro and Trade Gothic Std.
Photos on page 10, 43, 85 © Mike Oria, page 53 © Thinkstock/Jose Luis Peleaz Inc, page 55 © Mina Blyly-Strauss, page 73 © Thinkstock/Fuse, page 77 © Thinkstock/ David Sacks, page 93 © Thinkstock/Antonio_Diaz, page 97 © Thinkstock/ JoseGirarte, page 107 © Thinkstock/wavebreakmedia, page 131 © Thinkstock/ LucieHolloway, page 135 © Thinkstock/montiannoowong, page 154 © Thinkstock/ monkeybusinessimages, page 156 © Thinkstock/MonaMakela

Printed in the United States of America
22 21 20 19 18 17 16 15   1 2 3 4 5 6 7 8

Library of Congress Cataloging-in-Publication Data
Langworthy, Sara.
    Bridging the relationship gap : connecting with children facing adversity / Sara Langworthy. — First edition.
        pages   cm
    Includes bibliographical references and index.
    ISBN 978-1-60554-388-8 (pbk. : alk. paper) — ISBN 978-1-60554-389-5 (ebook)
1. Attachment behavior in children. 2. Interpersonal relations in children. 3. Early childhood education. I. Title.
    BF723.A75L36 2015
    155.4'192—dc23
                                                                        2015009364

Printed on acid-free paper

To my parents:
My first and best example of a consistent, caring, and
supportive relationship

Contents

Acknowledgments

This book, like any, was not a project completed in isolation. Many kudos, thanks, and champagne toasts are due to the following people for making this book a reality:

To Kyra Ostendorf, David Heath, Ashley Robinson, Alyssa Lochner, and the rest of the team at Redleaf Press for giving me the opportunity to do this crazy thing in the first place. To my editor, Danny Miller, and the rest of the editorial staff at Redleaf Press for keeping this book a reasonable length by keeping me concise and to the point, and for giving me thoughtful and helpful suggestions for how to make this book better along the way.

To my research heroes: Kathleen Thomas, Herb Pick, Ann Masten, Karen Cadigan, Rebecca Shlafer, Cathy Jordan, and so many others who have all inspired me through their passion and commitment to more deeply understanding the complex lives of children and families. To my colleagues at University of Minnesota Extension and the Children, Youth and Family Consortium for encouraging me to take on this challenge. To Shawn Dobbins, who made sure I got the best out of the deal before I even began to write. To Mike Oria, who let me share his beautiful images throughout this book. (See more of Mike's great work here: http://mikeoria.zenfolio.com.) To Dave, Dana, Isaac, and Abigail, who let me capture the beautiful simple moments of relationships in your family to share with others.

To the many care providers, professionals, and practitioners who shared their volumes of expertise on what it's like in the real world. Many of the practical suggestions in this book came from them. Thanks to Michele, Kamyala, Molly, and Rosemary for agreeing to talk freely about the incredible work that you do every day. Thanks to R. D., D. C., G. W., K. G., A. P., M. M., L. D., R. R., and I. T., whose stories helped pull me out of "researcher" mode and reminded me of the real children experiencing adversity every day. Special thanks to Stacey Bellows for talking me through what it's really like to be a care provider and for agreeing to review parts of this book to make sure I got things right.

To all the people who gave me feedback on this book. When I talked with my friend Sara about editing, she said, "You know, letting someone edit your writing is like letting them take a peek in your underwear drawer." So. True. I am so grateful that I have such wonderful colleagues whom I can trust to peek in my proverbial underwear drawer without fearing their ridicule. A million thanks to all of you who took time out of very busy lives to read drafts and provide constructive and supportive feedback. I'm looking at you, Sara Benning, Rebecca Shlafer, Judy Myers, Cari Michaels, and Stacey Bellows. You made this book better. Thank you.

And then there are all my friends, family, and colleagues, near and far, who cheered me on throughout the writing process with words of encouragement, hugs of support, and glasses of wine. I am especially indebted to:

My choir friends Marta, Kate, Christina, Katherine, and the rest of my National Lutheran Choir family who kept me singing and laughing throughout this process. Cari and Judy, the best colleagues a girl could ask for, whose constant encouragement throughout this entire journey has made writing a joy rather than a struggle. Amanda, Mark, Sara, Dave, Dana, Sara, Dave, Rebecca, Raquel, and Jason, who through chats, happy hours, and numerous board games nights helped remind me there's more to life than work. My parents-in-law Richard, Janet, and Margie, who, whether through shopping sprees to calm my nerves or hikes in the Arizona desert to stimulate my creativity, helped to keep me going when I needed motivation. Erin Arndt, who, like all best friends do, kept me humble and laughing. Sara Benning, my partner in crime, friend, and confidant, who talked me down from panic many times, and without whose constant source of support I would be lost. And of course, I can't forget my dogs, Bingley and Kaylee, who constantly gave slobbery dog kisses, kept my feet warm when I was typing for hours, and made sure I took breaks to throw the ball from time to time.

But there are three people I really owe this book to. Two are my parents, Paul and Joy Spencer, without whom I would not truly understand the power and value of caring, supportive, consistent relationships. I'm blessed to have a mother who picks up whenever I call, and whose many words of wisdom and constant support throughout the years have gotten me through life's ups and downs. My dad has been a constant source of quiet strength and humble perspective in my life, and has taught me that hard work and persistence really do pay off. As a team, my parents have taught me the value of drive, passion, curiosity, commitment, and love, and there aren't enough words to thank them for all they've done for me.

And last, but certainly not least, my incredible husband, Jason, who (and he'll tease me later for being mushy) is the love of my life. He reminds me daily that a sense of humor, a penchant for silliness, and a love of laughter are the things that make life worth living. Throughout the writing of this book, he endured many of my frustrated rants and anxious ramblings, and yet he was my unwavering source of support. He has never doubted me, and his calm, indefatigable confidence always gives me strength. He has kept me balanced, sane, and laughing through everything we've been through, a gift for which I could never thank him enough.

Hope in Spite of Brokenness

We need never be hopeless because we can never be irreparably broken.

JOHN GREEN

This quote from one of my favorite authors, John Green, was a constant mantra in my head while writing this book. Despite living in a world fraught with the pain and suffering of trauma and loss, we must cling to the hope of the possibility of change. The profound experiences of adversity—abuse, neglect, domestic violence, loss of a loved one, or homelessness—all leave their marks on the young children who experience them. Children who live through early adversity do not have words to express the pain and anguish of their experiences. They may not be able to ask for help from those around them, and they may cry out through their actions and emotions in ways that we don't understand. Such experiences may seem to change their lives irreparably.

It is enough to make anyone feel hopeless.

But the beauty of being human is that we constantly evolve and change. We have experiences every day that can alter the course of our lives to help us rebuild what was broken and rediscover what was lost. We, as humans, are never irreparably broken because our brains and bodies are built to change and adapt. And young children are often able to change more easily than the rest of us, which makes the earliest years of life the most full of hope.

The key to that hope is in relationships.

We've learned over the last few decades about the immense role that relationships play in shaping the brain and behavior (National Scientific Council on the Developing Child 2004b). Where scientists once believed that development of the brain was based solely on genetics and biology, we now know that the daily experiences and interactions with the people around us shape the way our brains are built. Strong, nurturing, and healthy relationships help to build solid foundations for later health and development (National Scientific Council on the Developing Child 2004b). The relationships that children experience during times of trauma and loss play a very important role in shaping the ultimate success of their recovery and healing. The presence of caring and responsive adults can help buffer children against the negative influences of early adversity.

As an early childhood professional, you can provide one of these essential relationships. This is a tall order when working with children who have experienced trauma or loss. Children who have endured traumatic experiences and grow up in environments where exposure to caring adults is limited are likely to be some of the most challenging children to work with. They may act out of control, disrupting the learning environment, or be so withdrawn you struggle to get them to come out of their shell. It may feel like you are perpetually taking one step forward, then two steps back. It may seem like there is a gaping precipice as big as the Grand Canyon between the two of you. Despite your repeated attempts to encourage them to join you on the other side, they refuse. Yet there are good reasons for their refusal, and your attempts are not made in vain.

But how do you bridge this relationship gap with children facing early adversity? How do you reach over the precipice to children on the other side and help them across? How do you build strong, secure relationships with children who have never experienced them before? This book will address many questions about what you as a professional can do to build strong relationships with the children in your care who have experienced trauma and loss. By combining the latest research with many practical guidelines, I hope to give you some thought-provoking ideas that might change the way you think about young children. This book is not meant to be an exhaustive examination of the topic, but it will provide background information about early childhood development research and what we've learned from practice about working with children who experience early adversity. This book will endeavor to answer some of the "why" questions behind the behaviors you may see in young children under stress. Why does it seem they can't control themselves? Why do their emotions overwhelm them? What happened to them to make them act this way? This book also seeks to provide information on additional resources and materials that you may find helpful in your daily practice. Furthermore, I hope that you are able to reflect on your own health and well-being as a care provider, and to explore the ways you can care for yourself so you are prepared to care for others.

In doing the background research for this book, I did a lot of reading, thinking, and listening. Through extensive reading, I learned about some of the "how-tos" of early care. In listening to care providers, I learned about the challenges faced on a daily basis in the care environment. Through preparing to write this book, I've gained a profound respect for the people like you who face a room full of energetic children every day with grace and a smile. It's an extraordinary gift.

In an effort to share that gift with others, I asked care providers and experts from across the country to provide their stories about working with children who have faced adversity. I did this through an online survey, as well as through many individual conversations with professionals. These stories were humbling to hear, and I am very grateful to those of you who shared your experiences with me. I have incorporated some of these stories throughout the book to highlight real-life experiences of those who care for children every day. The names of the children have been changed, as have some of the specific details, to protect the identities of those involved. Some of the stories are based on care providers' reflections, and others are my own reflections based on the circumstances of the shared story. Story sharers were named only if they chose to be, and they have given their approval to share their stories in this book.

This book is divided into two parts. The first part, "Relationships and Reality: What We Feel and What We Live," examines in the first two chapters the critical importance of early relationships for health and development. In chapters 3 and 4, you'll learn about the importance of context in shaping our lives and the devastating consequences that early adverse experiences of trauma and loss can have for young children. The second part, "Research and Response: What We Know, What We See, and What We Can Do," examines current research on some common types of traumatic experiences as well as strategies for working more effectively with children who have experienced trauma and loss. Lastly, in chapter 7, you'll learn about common methods of self-care and other ways to get involved with promoting the healthy development of young children everywhere. In addition, my website (www.drlangworthy.com) has more information and resources on all of the topics covered in the book. If you're using this book to teach a course, great companion videos, reports, and practical tip sheets are available through the website for use in your teaching. I encourage you to browse the website to deepen your learning and gather additional resources.

This book is not intended to be the magic solution to all your troubles. My hope is that you'll find that this resource brings research and practice to bear on the more difficult situations you may face in the early care environment. It is meant to help you think and act a little differently when you are working with children who experience extreme stress and adversity. In thinking about relationships, the brain, and the contexts in which children grow and learn, you can better understand where these children come from and how to connect with them. Armed with that knowledge, and with the skills and techniques to engage in productive ways with children who face trauma, you can have a positive impact on the lives of these children.

And so we begin where it all begins, with our very first and most important relationships.

PART 1

Relationships and Reality:
What We Feel and What We Live

I've learned that people will forget what you said, people will forget what you did, but people will never forget how you made them feel.

MAYA ANGELOU

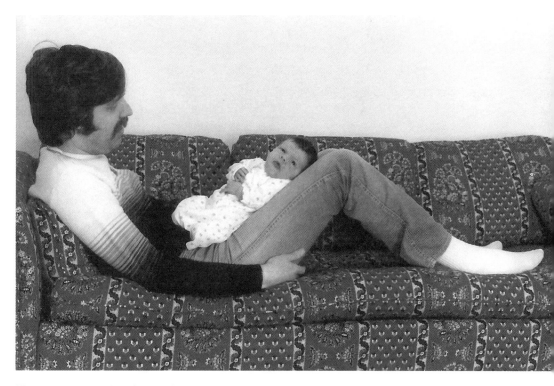

The author as a baby with her father.

1 How What We Feel Creates What We Know

Somebody's got to be crazy about that kid. That's number one.
First, last, and always.

URIE BRONFENBRENNER

 I open the door, a shrill cry greeting my ears. She's at it again. It happens this way most days lately. My wife likes to call it the "just that time of day" screaming fest. I'm told it's normal for babies to do this, but our ears could use a break from the sure to be future soprano in our midst.

"She's at it again, I see," I comment to my wife, who has our three-month-old daughter in her arms.

"Yes, and now I think it's your turn," she says, smiling, clearly relieved I've returned. I always did have perfect timing. I take my daughter from her mother and head to the living room, sit on the red couch, and lean back to let her lie on my outstretched legs.

She still screams, but I remain calm, holding her squirming body. I know she needs this daily afternoon cry, her wails seemingly a testament to the cruel reality of having little to no control over the rolling waves of emotions that overtake her for no rhyme or reason. But I sense she'll soon reach the dreaded point of no return.

So I look down into her face, my voice gentle, rhythmic, and calm: "Peace."

She stops crying abruptly, her teary eyes searching for my own. She seems surprised, almost perplexed; perplexed that she is crying, and perplexed that I am here, patiently looking down on her. I don't know if it's the rhythm of my voice, or just my refusal to let her screams disrupt my inner calm, but somehow it's like she understands. It's as if she senses my calm and latches on to it like a life preserver in the waves of tumultuous emotions that rock her tiny body. She understands that she is safe. No matter the intensity of her screams, I am there.

This is a conversation to be sure, but not one full of word-laden promises. Yet I sense there is shared understanding of them, nonetheless.

As her eyes search my face, her little thumb finds her mouth. Her hiccupping breaths begin to subside. Before long, she'll be ready for her dinner. But for now, it's just the two of us, a father and his daughter, saying so little, but understanding so much.

RELATIONSHIPS FIRST

This is a story I have heard often from my parents about my dad's inexplicable ability to calm me down from an infantile exhaustion-induced screaming fit with a simple word: "Peace." But it was never about the word, I suspect. I wasn't old enough to understand words yet. The calm, soothing voice and the solid presence of my dad communicated all that my infant self needed to know. His actions communicated safety, comfort, and love. They told me that he was someone I could rely on, always. Think about your relationships with the important people in your life. Maybe it's with a parent, a spouse, or a close friend. What is it about those relationships that make them important to you? Is it sharing common interests and experiences? Is it the feeling that you can count on these people no matter what? Is it the joy you get out of laughing together? Is it the comfort you feel when you are with them?

You probably rely on these relationships more than you even realize. In fact, those important relationships are such an integral part of your life that it is probably hard to imagine what life would be like without those close friends and family members. It's a part of our human nature to seek out those people around us who we believe will provide comfort, support, enjoyment, and love.

RELATIONSHIP ROOTS

Humans have a deeply rooted need for social connection. Early in human existence it became essential for humans to rely on one another for safety and security in order to thrive in an environment of constant threat. The necessity of relationships for survival begins at birth. Infants are born expecting and needing human interaction. Though we often think of infants as passive and helpless, their behaviors are actually biologically programmed to actively seek out interaction with adults (National Research Council and Institute of Medicine 2000). Throughout the years of growth from infancy into adulthood, youth rely heavily on the adults surrounding them to provide stability, safety, and guidance. It is during those years of infancy, childhood, and adolescence that strong emotional bonds with other humans form, change, and grow. These relationships teach us about our world and what to expect from it. These bonds are essential for successful growth and development into adulthood (National Scientific Council on the Developing Child 2004b).

Human babies are not alone in seeking important relationships with others. Some animal species display similar tendencies. Research with ducks, dogs, goats, and monkeys has demonstrated that early in life many types of animals seek comfort and nurturance from an adult figure (Bowlby 1982). One of the most well-known and striking demonstrations of this involved baby monkeys who were given the option of spending time with a "wire mother," which only provided food, and a "cloth mother," which was an object wrapped in cloth meant to simulate a mother monkey. Despite the biological need for food, the baby monkeys spent most of their time seeking comfort from the cloth mother rather than obtaining food from the wire mother. Furthermore, when loud noises or frightening objects scared these monkeys, they clung fiercely to the cloth mother to seek comfort. These monkeys viewed the cloth mother as a source of comfort and safety (Bowlby 1982; Harlow 1958).

Similarly, human babies are born seeking this kind of connection and comfort from the people around them. When they are upset, being soothed by an adult helps them to become calm. Infants actively seek out responses from adults around them by cooing or squealing. These early relationships have been shown to play an integral part in brain development and have been linked to cognitive, social, and emotional outcomes later in life (National Scientific Council on the Developing Child 2004a; Shonkoff and Garner 2012). Researchers, practitioners, and parents have come to call these important relationships between infants and adult caregivers *attachment relationships*.

THE GIVE AND TAKE OF EARLY RELATIONSHIPS

The term *attachment* describes the close bonds between humans that stem from seeking comfort, stability, and protection from one another (Bowlby 1982; National Research Council and Institute of Medicine 2000). Traditionally, this term is used to describe the nature of the relationship between children and their caregivers. Attachment research began with very young children and their parents. However, there is also a large body of research examining attachment relationships throughout adolescence and adulthood (National Research Council and Institute of Medicine 2000). The attachment relationship between a caregiver and child occurs through the process of back-and-forth interactions, sometimes called *serve-and-return* interactions. Through these daily exchanges, babies are able to learn about the stability and predictability of their environment, and learn to trust the caregiver as a source of comfort and safety (National Scientific Council on the Developing Child 2004b).

The Role of Serve-and-Return Interactions in Attachment

Serve-and-return interactions are daily exchanges that are the basis of early communication between the baby and parent. Consistent and positive exchanges help to build strong relationships between parents and their children. A serve-and-return interaction is like a game of tennis. One player serves the ball, hitting it across the net to the other player. The second player then returns the serve, sending the ball back across the net to the first player. Interactions between children and caregivers are very similar. For example, a baby might coo or squeal to get her mother's attention. The mother then returns that interaction by looking at the baby and smiling. The baby might then point to a dog outside the window, and the mother might look at the dog and say, "Oh, look, it's a dog!" These types of simple back and forth interactions tell the baby that the adult is engaged with her and receptive to her needs. It is the build-up of these interactions over time that helps construct an attachment relationship (National Scientific Council on the Developing Child 2004b).

When these serve-and-return interactions are largely positive and responsive, the result is a solid foundation for secure attachment. The key attributes of a positive, or *secure*, attachment relationship involve the caregiver providing safety and security to the infant. In secure attachments, babies learn that their emotional needs will be met and that their caregivers will provide consistent care and safety—a "safe base" from which they can freely explore the world around them. Babies who exhibit secure attachments to their caregivers are likely to explore their surroundings but will return regularly to their caregivers to "check in." When they are frightened, securely attached babies will seek comfort from their caregivers, and the caregivers will respond soothingly to help calm them (National Research Council and Institute of Medicine 2000).

Research suggests that secure attachments in infancy are linked to a variety of positive health and behavioral outcomes later in life. Children with more secure relationships with caregivers are likely to have increased empathy, be more insightful of other people's feelings and thoughts, and engage in more cooperative interactions with peers later in childhood. In addition, these strong relationships build a basis of language development and set a foundation for more successful cognitive and academic outcomes (National Scientific Council on the Developing Child 2004b).

Not all types of attachment relationships are positive. Indeed, secure attachments are most common, but relationships between children and caregivers can become strained or even destructive. In these relationships, children do not receive consistent messages of comfort and security, often causing them to learn mixed messages about their environment. To use the tennis metaphor, it is as if the second player didn't return the ball back over the net, or perhaps hit the ball too hard to a spot where the first player couldn't return it. The game quickly turns from friendly to frustrating. In the context of early relationships, babies may seek out adults' responses by squealing or cooing, and if adults do not respond, respond negatively, or are inconsistent in their responses, babies will not receive messages of stability and comfort (National Scientific Council on the Developing Child 2004b). Instead, babies learn that seeking comfort results in either receiving no comfort or being hurt by the caregiver. The lack of consistent, positive serve-and-return interactions can lead to *insecure* attachments. In these interactions, adults may respond to children's babbles or cries with anger or indifference. When caregivers neglect to respond, babies may try even harder to engage the adults, perhaps leading to a negative outburst from the adults. Eventually, babies learn that these caregivers are not consistently responsive to their needs, or worse, that the caregivers are the source of some threat to them. They may then completely disengage from the caregivers or be distressed by their presence (National Research Council and Institute of Medicine 2000).

Of course, insecure attachments are not the same as the occasional missed response to a baby's excited giggle. Insecure attachments are built on repeatedly inconsistent or negative and hurtful responses to the child. All caregivers have days when they aren't at their best. Insecure attachments form when parents have their worst day every day, and as a result cannot be the responsive, caring adults that babies require to meet their needs. Yet, even when infants learn that their caregivers are inconsistent in their care and responsiveness, these babies still gain important emotional support from the presence of the caregivers that they do not get from the presence of just any other adult (National Research Council and Institute of Medicine 2000). Thus, primary caregivers are still crucial to the growth and development of their children and are not easily replaced by other adults.

The "Strange Situation" Experiment

Researchers have developed creative ways to measure the attachment relationship between a young child and caregiver. The classic study of differences in attachment patterns is called the "Strange Situation" experiment developed by Mary Ainsworth in the 1970s (Ainsworth et al. [1978] 2014; Bowlby 1982). In this experiment, a young child (one to two years of age) and a parent or guardian are brought into a research laboratory room containing toys and are encouraged to play. Then, an adult that the child does not know enters the room and converses with the parent. After a few minutes, the parent is instructed to leave the room. Researchers observe the young child's behavior at the caregiver's departure. Children are typically distressed when their parent leaves the room. The other adult stranger offers comfort to the child if the child is very upset but otherwise remains a neutral presence. After a short time, the parent returns to the room, and researchers observe the characteristics of the reunion between the parent and child (Ainsworth et al. [1978] 2014). In general, researchers gauge the child's level of exploration of the new environment, the child's reaction to the parent leaving, the child's anxiety response to the strange adult, and the child's reunion behaviors with the parent. The child's response to the parent's return is the most telling measure of attachment security.

In a secure attachment relationship, the young child may show some anxiety when first entering the room, but at the parent's coaxing and encouragement may begin to explore the room and engage in play with the parent. When a new adult enters the room, the child may seem unsure at first, but once determining from the parent that the other adult is not a threat, may even play with the other adult. Once the parent leaves the room, a child with a secure attachment style will likely express distress and cry for the caregiver to return. Her source of comfort and safety has left her in a potentially scary situation, leaving her upset and uncertain. The child will likely eventually calm down but may also remain observably unhappy while the parent is gone. However, once the parent returns, the child will eagerly seek comfort and reunion with the caregiver. She is clearly happy to see the caregiver and will seek comfort and solace from the caregiver immediately. The key to the secure attachment style is that the child is comforted by the parent's return (Ainsworth et al. [1978] 2014).

In an insecure attachment relationship, this pattern of behavior looks very different. In general, a child with an insecure attachment style may not seek to engage the parent in play initially. She may not even seek interaction with the parent at all during the first stage of the experiment. Then when the parent leaves, the child with an insecure attachment style may become upset, much like a child with a secure attachment. Conversely, the child may not even notice or seem to care that the parent has left the room. When the other adult offers to comfort the child, the child may receive comfort, avoid the adult and remain distressed alone, or seem ambivalent about the presence of the other adult. Interestingly, in some cases, the child with an insecure attachment style may seem to gain as much comfort from the presence of the other adult as she does from her parent. When the parent returns, a variety of responses may occur. The child may seek comfort from the parent but then physically pull away on contact. She may approach the parent and then stop and resort to crying in place rather than approaching the parent further. In some cases, the child may not even seem to care that the parent has returned. Unlike the children with secure attachment styles, children who have insecure attachment styles do not effectively use their caregivers as a source of support and comfort to ease their distress. It is these responses to this scenario that are telling indicators of potential insecurity of the attachment bond between the child and parent (Ainsworth et al. [1978] 2014).

Attachment patterns have been categorized by researchers into four primary categories: secure, insecure-avoidant, insecure-ambivalent/resistant, and insecure-disorganized (Ainsworth et al. [1978] 2014; Main and Solomon 1990). Infants with *secure* attachment styles, as described above, clearly seek comfort and support from a parent and will willingly participate in exploratory behaviors with the parent present. Within the context of the Strange Situation experiment, on a parent's return, children seek out comfort to ease their distress, and the parent's presence has a soothing effect (Ainsworth et al. [1978] 2014). It is important to remember that these behaviors are observed primarily in very young children (one to two years of age), and these attachment patterns will look different in older children.

Children with *insecure-avoidant* attachment styles tend to explore a new environment considerably less than their peers, even in the presence of the parent. One of the hallmark behaviors of insecure-avoidant attachment is the child's apparent ambivalence about the parent's presence or absence. That is, they do not seem to care if their parent is with them or not. They express little distress at the parent's departure and little comfort or relief at the parent's return (Ainsworth et al. [1978] 2014). Within the context of the early care environment, this may be most noticed at the end of the day when parents come to pick up their children. Typically, children become excited to see their parents and will eagerly engage with them. However, children with more insecure-avoidant patterns of attachment may not seem to care or be excited to see their parents.

Children with *insecure-ambivalent/resistant* patterns of attachment will also tend to explore very little, even in the presence of their parent. They also express some distress or wariness at the presence of the other adult. Interestingly, these children tend to notice their parent's return (unlike children with the insecure-avoidant pattern), but they may express noticeably angry behaviors toward the adult. Conversely, they may seek out comfort from their parent through more passive means (crying on the floor) rather than actively approaching them upon their return (running to parent, demanding to be picked up). In the early care context, these children may be visibly upset or angry at their parent's return instead of having a joyful reunion (Ainsworth et al. [1978] 2014).

Years after Mary Ainsworth developed the Strange Situation experiment, researcher Mary Main suggested that a fourth subtype of attachment exists: *insecure-disorganized* attachment. This attachment style is the least defined and most ambiguous. Yet Mary Main argued that insecure-disorganized attachment exists when children do not seem to have a pattern of behavior consistent with expressing discomfort at a parent's departure or seeking comfort from the parent's return. Instead, children with insecure-disorganized attachments may seem to express fear in the presence of the caregiver or engage in odd behaviors that do not indicate any strategies for how to seek comfort from adults (Howes and Ritchie 2002; Main and Solomon 1990). In the context of early care, these children may exhibit many challenging behaviors. You should certainly be aware of children who appear fearful at a parent's return, as this may indicate a more serious problem. Research in the last ten to fifteen years has begun to examine insecure-disorganized attachment styles more systematically to attempt to articulate these types of behaviors more concretely.

It is again worth noting that it is the consistency of these types of reactions that are most important. Children may have days when they are more upset than on others because of things unrelated to the security of their attachment relationships with their parents. However, if a child consistently responds in fear or avoidance of a parent, concern may be warranted. As a care provider, you will see that being aware of the patterns of how young children respond to their parents can be a useful tool in understanding children's challenging behaviors in the early care environment.

Attachment in the Early Care Environment

To many early care providers, challenging good-byes and tearful reunions are common scenarios. In fact, the child's stress at a parent's departure is a common part of every early care environment. But it is the coping through that stressful experience that is a marker for the child's attachment security. The ways that a child copes with these challenges also shift over time, making it a dynamic, ever-changing process. Attachment is not a static construct. It changes and grows with the child and caregiver; always effected by the surrounding environment (National Scientific Council on the Developing Child 2004b).

Furthermore, parents or guardians do not provide the only important relationship in a young child's life. Indeed, early care providers often develop strong attachment relationships with children in their care (Howes and Ritchie 2002). Interestingly, the type of attachment relationship children have with their primary caregivers does not necessarily determine the type of attachment relationship they will have with care providers or any other adults. Children often develop different types of attachment relationships with different adults in their lives. That is, if a child has an insecure attachment with his father, he might have a secure attachment with a preschool teacher. Care providers have a tremendous opportunity to support and promote the development of these important early relationships.

What do different types of attachment look like in an early care environment? Children expressing a secure attachment pattern will tend to seek comfort from a trusted adult when they are upset or hurt. They are more likely to ask for help when they need it, easily follow instructions and directions, transition smoothly between activities throughout the day, and share in activities and exploration with the provider (Howes and Ritchie 2002). The nuances of differences in behavior of the subtypes of insecure attachments often require a keen observer. In general, children with an insecure attachment style may be more difficult to work with because of their challenging behaviors. Unfortunately, behavioral problems are often a noticeable consequence of insecure attachments. Children with insecure-avoidant attachment styles tend to turn away and reject comfort from providers and are rated by teachers as more aggressive and likely to withdraw from situations (Howes and Ritchie 2002). Conversely, children who express insecure-ambivalent/resistant attachment styles tend to be both excessively dependent on the care provider while also being difficult to work with. These children tend to be fearful and upset when the care provider leaves, but are also likely to display demanding and aggressive behaviors with the care provider. Children with insecure-disorganized attachment styles are perhaps the most confusing children to work with, as their behaviors are inconsistent and difficult to predict. These children seem to have no clear patterns of interacting with the care provider, and thus it is difficult for providers to develop connections with these children because of the unpredictability of their actions (Howes and Ritchie 2002).

When working with children with challenging behaviors in the early care environment, it is not important to know which subtype of insecure attachment may be a root cause of the behaviors. However, understanding that the behaviors you see may be a result of some underlying relationship challenges with primary caregivers can be useful in exploring how to most effectively work with young children. Furthermore, exposure to stress and trauma, in addition to affecting children directly, can also disrupt important attachment relationships with caregivers (see chapters 2 and 4).

WHAT ATTACHMENT MEANS FOR LATER DEVELOPMENT

Attachment relationships are not only important for providing safety and security to young children during early life. These relationships also provide crucial foundations for physical health, as well as cognitive, social, and emotional development later in life.

Exploration and Discovery

Children use relationships with trusted adults to gauge the safety of their surroundings. Young children are very skilled at reading their caregivers' behaviors and emotions, and they use this emotional information to help assess the safety of the environment. One classic experiment that highlights the importance of the caregiver's emotions in infants' exploration is the "Visual Cliff" experiment. In this classic experiment, infants are placed on a plexiglass table with a high-contrast checkerboard pattern underneath. On one half of the table, the checkerboard pattern is directly under the plexiglass. On the other half, the checkerboard is draped four feet below the plexiglass, simulating a drop-off, or "visual cliff." However, because the plexiglass can hold the weight of the infant, the drop-off is merely simulated. Though babies are comfortable crawling on the part of the table with the checkerboard directly under the plexiglass, they tend to avoid crawling on the part of the table that simulates the drop off (Gibson and Walk 1960). However, when encouraged by their caregiver through positive emotions (smiles, encouragement) to cross the table in spite of the drop-off, many infants attempt to make the crossing. Conversely, if caregivers express fear or concern, the child will more likely stay on the "safe" part of the table (Sorce et al. 1985). This type of interaction is seen throughout experiments that stretch infants' skills and comfort levels. Caregivers' expressions of emotions are crucial in helping infants assess threat and understand the safety of the surrounding environment.

The ability to learn about threats and safety in the environment through interaction with caregivers builds a strong sense of trust between caregivers and their children. This trust furthers the development of a child's confidence with exploring other unknown situations. These early experiences build a strong foundation for later learning and exploration in school and social situations throughout life (National Scientific Council on the Developing Child 2004b).

Emotional Development

Caregivers' emotions play an important role not only in signaling safety or threat to young children but also in teaching them how to understand, communicate, and regulate their own emotions. Responsive caregivers may treat children's emotional outbursts as a chance to talk through their feelings in a way that helps them feel understood. Even when children don't understand language, speaking in soothing tones can be helpful. When the caregiver maintains a sense of calm when a child feels emotionally out of control, the caregiver is communicating responsiveness and comfort (National Research Council and Institute of Medicine 2000). For example, a mother might hold her screaming infant and calmly speak in soothing tones, or might tell her angry two-year-old, "Natalie, I know you are angry with me, but I'm going to stay right here with you." These words and actions convey that even when the child is upset, the caregiver will be a source of support throughout the emotional roller coaster.

Caregivers who are stressed and struggle to regulate their own emotions may have difficulty responding constructively to a child's emotional outbursts. Sometimes caregivers respond by yelling, scolding, or physically shaking the child when a child is emotional. Think about the mother described above. Imagine she speaks angrily to her crying infant or yells at her two-year-old, "Natalie! Stop yelling or you'll be in big trouble." This type of response may serve only to increase the child's emotionality, because she may interpret her mother's emotion as cause for further alarm. Caregivers' highly emotional responses may exacerbate rather than curb the child's disruptive behaviors. Before long, the interaction can turn into a spiraling cycle of uncontrollable emotion for both caregiver and child. However, working with caregivers on finding healthy ways to manage their own emotions and be more responsive and soothing in their interactions with their children can be extremely beneficial in helping them build more stable relationships. When caregivers become more responsive and emotionally calm, it teaches children that even when they feel out of control, they are safe with their caregivers (National Research Council and Institute of Medicine 2000; National Scientific Council on the Developing Child 2009).

These calming and responsive reactions of caregivers over time help strengthen children's ability to regulate their own emotions. By the time they reach preschool, children are then more adept at understanding, expressing, and talking about emotions in a much more complex way (National Scientific Council on the Developing Child 2004a). Caregiver responsiveness helps children begin to understand complex emotions and also use language to describe their feelings. In fact, children of caregivers who provide consistent emotional stability tend to be much more able to express their emotions appropriately later in childhood (National Scientific Council on the Developing Child 2004a). Children more capable of emotional understanding and control tend to be more cooperative and empathetic with peers, have a stronger sense of conscience, and have more skilled ways of handling conflict (National Research Council and Institute of Medicine 2000; National Scientific Council on the Developing Child 2004a).

As they learn about emotion through interactions with responsive caregivers, children begin to develop self-regulation, or the ability to control behaviors in appropriate ways. The ability to regulate emotions and behaviors is crucial for success in structured environments such as school. The foundations of self-regulation are developed early through the serve-and-return interactions that young babies experience with their caregivers. The development of self-regulation continues throughout early life as children learn how to appropriately understand and express emotions and control their behaviors (National Research Council and Institute of Medicine 2000). Young children learn these skills of self-regulation through these coaching interactions with caregivers who are consistently responsive to their physical and emotional needs. The seeds of the emotions and behaviors children express later in life are cultivated through these early interactions with adults.

Building Self-Concept

In the mid-twentieth century, psychologist Lev Vygotsky proposed that how caregivers supported their children's learning was an important factor in development. Caregivers who engage with their children in challenging activities without taking over, while providing adequate coaching and encouragement, can help foster positive social skills in their children (National Research Council and Institute of Medicine 2000). Conversely, some children have parents who take over a problem and provide a solution because it's easier than waiting for their children to figure out a solution on their own. This tendency to take over can communicate to children that they are not capable of solving the problem, and can result in lower self-esteem and feelings of helplessness. Conversely, some children have caregivers who refuse to help them solve complex problems or provide any input or coaching at all. In those situations, children may not feel supported in their explorations, resulting in increased frustration or apathy. Instead, caregivers who are able to provide a balance of coaching and encouragement without taking over provide children with what scientists call *scaffolding*.

Much like scaffolding's purpose on a building is to provide support and structure, scaffolding in early life is the process by which caregivers provide necessary input to help children discover solutions on their own. It's the process of working together with children that helps build their confidence, skills, learning, and later cooperation with others (National Research Council and Institute of Medicine 2000). For example, if Paul is playing a memory matching game and his father helps him by cuing him with phrases such as "Do you remember where the other elephant card was?" and "Maybe you should try this row of cards," Paul receives not only useful information for solving the problem at hand, but also feels supported in that endeavor. Conversely, if Paul's father were to take over and do all the matching for him, Paul would likely lose interest in the game entirely and withdraw. If his father did not help him at all with the game, Paul might become frustrated and quit playing entirely.

Parents are not the only people to provide these types of learning experiences. In fact, many of the games and activities recommended for early care environments naturally use this idea of scaffolding. Some activities may be challenging tasks for children, but with the assistance of a care provider, the tasks are manageable and children can master new skills. Encouraging children to remain engaged in challenging tasks can be difficult, especially if they are accustomed to adults taking over or not helping them at all. However, by offering gentle encouragement and providing a variety of opportunities to master challenging tasks, care providers can help children learn problem-solving skills. Furthermore, the sense of pride and self-confidence built by these learning experiences is important for later learning and social relationships (National Research Council and Institute of Medicine 2000).

Importance of Peer Relationships

In addition to providing children an opportunity to learn, explore, and build self-regulation, early relationships with sensitive caregivers also help build social skills important for interacting with peers later in life. Regulating emotions is a major component of successful peer interaction. That is, children who are able to express emotions appropriately are more likely to be sensitive and understanding of their peers' emotions. Empathy and sensitivity are core components of lasting friendships (National Scientific Council on the Developing Child 2004b).

Furthermore, in navigating early relationships, children learn core concepts about resolving conflict with others. A caregiver's responsiveness in handling conflict with a child, or between children, helps children begin to understand and handle conflict in appropriate ways. These skills of cooperation and conflict resolution can positively affect how children interact with their peers (National Research Council and Institute of Medicine 2000). Fostering these skills early in life through responsive caregiving is important for later development of positive social relationships and success in school (National Scientific Council on the Developing Child 2004a, 2004b).

CULTURE AND RELATIONSHIPS

Attachment relationships do not develop in a vacuum. There are many characteristics in the surrounding environment that may influence the way early relationships develop. One of the most important factors that influences how attachment relationships develop is culture (National Research Council and Institute of Medicine 2000). Culture affects individual caregivers, families, communities, and learning environments. Thus, it is impossible to understand early childhood development without considering culture.

In recent years, there has been more exploration of culture as an important factor in development, but it is outside the scope of this book to exhaustively explore the many varied developmental nuances of children from different cultures. However, it is important to note that differences in how relationships develop in various cultures may influence the way children and their caregivers interact. Because our understanding of attachment comes from primarily western European cultural backgrounds, there may be cultural nuances that are lost, or worse, misinterpreted, about the quality of attachment relationships across cultures. Early care providers are facing unprecedented numbers of children from a variety of cultural backgrounds, each with its own differences and complexities. It is important to understand that the ways children express their attachments may vary greatly because of their own traditions and cultural experiences. Furthermore, those variations do not necessarily indicate poor attachment relationships. Taking the step to learn more about the children and families you work with is imperative in creating a positive and supportive care environment. It is necessary to always consider children's culture, environment, family, and personal experiences when interpreting their behaviors.

CONCLUSIONS

Throughout the early years, children learn extensively about the world around them through their relationships with others. The quality and consistency of those relationships is one of the most important factors in children's early lives. In short, relationships matter. They are the context in which other learning occurs. These early relationships with caregivers build important connections in the brain, facilitate the ability of young children to control their behaviors, and support children's ongoing learning throughout their lives.

LINGERING QUESTIONS

➤ **Can a child be attached to more than one person?** Yes! In fact, young children rely on having a few key primary attachment relationships with people around them. These may be parents, grandparents, or other care providers. If you're spending a lot of time with a child as a care provider, you could be one of his primary attachment figures. In addition, there is no evidence to suggest that children having secure relationships with multiple caregivers is damaging to, or interferes with, the strength of children's relationships with their primary caregivers (National Scientific Council on the Developing Child 2004b).

➤ **What about fathers?** Attachment has largely been studied by examining the relationship between the mother and child. This should not be taken to mean that fathers do not have attachment relationships with their children—quite the opposite! In fact, research indicates that the importance of the father-child bond is as important as the relationship between mother and child (National Research Council and Institute of Medicine 2000).

➤ **Do children have different attachment relationships with different people?** Yes. Children may have secure attachment relationships with some people and insecure attachments with others. However, if children have a strong primary relationship that is secure in nature, they will likely have fewer insecure relationships with others (National Research Council and Institute of Medicine 2000).

➤ **Do attachment relationships change over time?** Yes. Attachment is not a static concept. In fact, children may have insecure attachments with their primary caregivers early in life, but at other times of their lives they may have securer attachments. In addition, these relationships are not more or less important at particular stages of life, but the impact of those relationships may vary based on age (National Scientific Council on the Developing Child 2004b).

2 How What We Feel Builds the Brain

The Brain - is wider than the Sky -
For - put them side by side -
The one the other will contain
With ease - and You - beside -
The Brain is deeper than the sea -
For - hold them - Blue to Blue -
The one the other will absorb -
As Sponges - Buckets - do -

EMILY DICKINSON

Though you might not often think about it, everything that you see, think, and do is a result of how your brain makes sense of the world around you. Your brain acts as a filter, sifting through the large amounts of information that constantly surround you. At any given moment, your brain is processing multiple sights, sounds, smells, touches, and thoughts. Your brain helps to process what information is important for you to pay attention to and what can just fall away into the background noise of your surroundings. It takes in information, calculates probabilities, creates expectations of particular outcomes, and adapts possible behaviors based on those outcomes. Your brain takes all new information that you learn and links it to existing connections, creating an intricate web of information. This process of building the brain, though honed throughout life, is especially informed by early experiences.

Like a spider builds a web, the brain constructs an intricate web of connections through constant interaction with the surrounding environment. The brain is predisposed to pick up on patterns, regularities, and constants that help to build a structure of probabilities. Our brains learn to predict certain outcomes based on the surrounding information and create behaviors that are most likely to result in survival. These connections that the brain builds early in life become strengthened across the life span. Sometimes these connections are broken, or the paths change as the brain adapts to new information. But the foundations on which all future growth and development are built are laid in the earliest years of life.

BRAIN DEVELOPMENT: THE BASICS

One of the most common analogies about early brain development is that it is like a construction zone. Imagine you're building your own dream house. You've been thinking about it for years, planning in your mind exactly where things will go and how it all will look. You've worked with an architect to draw up blueprints and plans so that the construction workers will know exactly what to do. The construction team then takes those blueprints and begins working—starting with the foundation, making sure the base of the house is solid before building anything else. Then they start building on top of that foundation, creating rooms, building walls, and putting in plumbing and electrical systems. Throughout the process, there are occasional hiccups and unexpected changes to the blueprints because of the land or the materials or cost. These environmental factors, which you couldn't predict early on, alter the way the plans play out. But if you planned things well and the construction workers built a strong foundation, these changes are likely to be fairly minor. However, if you had an architect who cut corners or a construction team who didn't have all the information they needed to build a solid foundation, you're more likely to have much bigger problems on your hands.

You can think about brain development in the same way. So often when people think about early brain development, they immediately think of a baby's first year, development that begins once a baby is born. However, substantial development occurs before birth, during the prenatal period, that is important for laying down strong foundations for later health and development.

Typical Early Brain Development

Even before a woman knows she's pregnant, a tremendous amount of growth and change begin in her body. Once a sperm meets an egg and cells begin dividing, the genetic code begins creating the cells that will one day be a baby. Throughout the mother's pregnancy, or the prenatal period, tremendous growth of cells, organs, and physical features takes place in the fetus. When brain development happens in a typical fashion, a number of steps occur. First, the brain cells are created. Then they must travel to where they are supposed to be. These cells then undergo structural development, creating the necessary parts to enable connections with other cells (National Research Council and Institute of Medicine 2000). Throughout this process, the construction workers, or brain cells, begin putting the genetic blueprints into action, and the foundation of brain development begins.

Prenatal brain development is heavily dependent on how the genetic code is expressed. The idea that human genes are set and unchangeable was one of the biggest early misconceptions of the scientific study of the human body. More recently, scientists have begun to understand that genes cannot only be expressed or "turned on or off" in different ways, but environmental factors can determine whether genes are expressed at all (National Scientific Council on the Developing Child 2010). Think of it as a dimming light switch. You can switch the light all the way on to get full light and all the way off to get complete darkness. But you can also use the dimmer switch to vary the strength of the light. Gene expression can happen in a similar way. Complex and interacting factors in the environment and the body determine which genes are switched on and off, and how powerfully they are expressed.

Still more complex is the idea that even though a gene is turned on, a particular outcome may not absolutely occur. Instead, scientists now talk about how certain genes might "predispose," or increase the chances that you will achieve a certain condition. For example, a pair of identical twins might express slight differences, despite having the same genetic makeup. One might be a little taller; one might have slightly curlier hair. These attributes, though linked to specific genes, can be affected by factors in the environment. Scientists use the term *epigenome* to describe the genetic "software system" that tells your genetic "hardware" what genes to express and in what ways (National Scientific Council on the Developing Child 2010). Essentially, different experiences in the environment can lead to changes in the epigenome, which in turn determine how different genes are expressed. In the identical twins, for example, there may be factors in their surrounding environment that influence the twins' individual epigenomes to "dim" to varying degrees the genes responsible for height or hair, resulting in different expressions of those characteristics. This process of building the epigenome is ongoing. It begins before the infant is born and continues across the life span. However, the prenatal period is very important for the beginnings of building the epigenome and the brain. There are many external factors that can cause this early brain development to go off course.

When Things Go Wrong

There are many things that can cause disruptions to the process of brain development before a baby is even born. Issues such as genetic abnormalities or other biological factors can cause severe impairment or the death of the fetus. These types of abnormalities, though potentially devastating, are not usually within the control of the mother (National Scientific Council on the Developing Child 2010).

However, there are other common disruptions of prenatal development that are, to a degree, dependent on the mother's economic, social, and health status. Using drugs and alcohol, and experiencing malnutrition, nutrient deficiencies, or maternal stress have all been linked to problems in prenatal development (National Scientific Council on the Developing Child 2006, 2007). Especially during certain windows of development, such as the first three months after conception, using drugs and alcohol can have devastating effects on the health and development of a baby. Interestingly, above all other recreational drugs, alcohol has been found to have the most substantial and long-lasting effects on early brain development. Excessive alcohol use during these first few months of pregnancy can severely affect brain cells, organs, and the cardiovascular and digestive systems of the fetus (National Scientific Council on the Developing Child 2006). Fetal alcohol syndrome (FAS), a medical condition involving deficiencies in multiple organ systems, is due to excessive alcohol exposure during the prenatal period. FAS can have destructive effects on the child's learning, growth, and social development. Though potentially not as devastating as alcohol use, the use of other drugs, including nicotine, during pregnancy can have similar effects on the fetus, disrupting typical brain development at crucial points (National Scientific Council on the Developing Child 2006). The use of drugs and alcohol during pregnancy is relatively controllable, but in the case of severe addictions, it may be more difficult for the mother to curb the negative effects of drug use.

Other conditions that impact prenatal health, such as malnutrition or nutrient deficiencies, are often dependent on the mother's access to healthy food, clean water, necessary vitamins, and adequate medical care. Malnutrition or nutrient deficiencies can severely impact the growth and development of the fetus, affecting the brain, organs, and physiological systems (National Scientific Council on the Developing Child 2010). Furthermore, there are cases in which the mother's body reacts to the fetus in a way that alters which nutrients are made available to the baby. For example, maternal diabetes may lead to iron deficiency in babies, which has been linked to poor cognitive outcomes later in the child's life (National Research Council and Institute of Medicine 2000). The importance of promoting healthy choices and the availability of sufficient medical care during pregnancy cannot be overstated.

Premature birth is another factor that can have long-lasting implications on children's lives. The important growth of brain and organ systems is not fully complete when infants are born prematurely. This places premature infants at increased risk of disruption to the development of brain and body because they are suddenly severed from the mother's body before they are ready. It is remarkable that with the advances in modern medicine, not only are premature babies more likely to survive despite these adverse conditions, but they are more likely to achieve fairly typical functioning later in life. However, extreme prematurity (born between twenty-four and twenty-eight weeks) has been linked to diverse physical, cognitive, emotional, and social difficulties later in life. Moreover, prematurity is often linked to other life factors such as poverty, poor health, and stress (National Research Council and Institute of Medicine 2000). A host of factors, including extreme stress, drug use, and poor nutrition impact mothers and may result in infants being born prematurely. Availability of adequate health care and prenatal support and education for pregnant women is an important public health concern.

Maternal stress can lead to premature birth, but it can also affect the basic brain development of the baby. Research in animals has shown that when pregnant mothers experience high levels of consistent stress during the pregnancy, babies exhibit prolonged stress responses later in life (National

Scientific Council on the Developing Child 2010). In other words, when a pregnant mother experiences high levels of stress because of situations such as living in an unsafe neighborhood, experiencing consistent discord with the family, or facing pressures of unemployment, her body's response to that stress can affect the baby and change the way the brain's stress system is built in a potentially detrimental way. Public efforts that work to reduce stress on pregnant women and their families through enhancing neighborhood safety or increasing access to suitable employment opportunities can positively affect the health and development of their babies.

Earliest Days

You might think that once a baby is born, the basic building of the brain is complete, but, in fact, it is far from finished. Even when all the brain cells have migrated to their specified locations and have begun to branch out and connect with other neurons, these cells require input. They are primed and ready to begin changing and making connections as they receive information from the outside world. Indeed, the prenatal period merely begins the process of putting the blueprint into action. There are still many ways the blueprint can and will change based on input from the surrounding environment (National Scientific Council on the Developing Child 2010).

One of the long-standing debates in the scientific community is whether babies are born with the total number of brain cells they will have for their entire lives. Growth of new brain cells later in life was once believed impossible, but more recent research suggests that certain parts of the brain may be able to produce new brain cells even after birth (National Research Council and Institute of Medicine 2000; Pathania and Bordey 2013). This discovery changes the way researchers think about the human brain and its ability to change and grow over the life span. However, even in light of these findings, most of the neurons a person will ever have are present at birth. These neurons are primed and ready to receive important environmental input to begin changing and growing by reaching out to other neurons to form important communication networks. These connections are formed through a process called *synaptogenesis.*

Synaptogenesis is the growth of the synapses, which are the connection points between neurons. Synapses are the gaps that exist between two connecting neurons where the brain's chemicals, called neurotransmitters, pass back and forth to communicate signals. When babies are born, they do not have many connections developed between these neurons. But during the first few years of life, the brain goes through a major period of synaptogenesis, producing billions of connections across the brain (National Research Council and Institute of Medicine 2000). Though the peak of this process is in childhood, in some areas of the brain this process may continue well into adolescence and early adulthood. This tremendous period of growth

DEFINITIONS

- **Neuron:** The tiny cells that make up the brain. Neurons connect with one another through chemical signals to transmit information across the brain.

- **Synapse:** The gap that exists between two neurons. Signals jump between neurons over the synapse through releasing chemicals.

- **Neurotransmitters:** The chemicals that facilitate communication between neurons. These chemicals travel over the synapse to enable communication between neurons. Common neurotransmitters are dopamine, norepinephrine, and serotonin.

- **Brain networks:** Like a computer network, the brain has locations that are interconnected to make certain senses and behaviors possible. These systems are often wired together early in life.

- **Cortisol:** A stress hormone released by the body during times of fear, anxiety, or danger. Though some cortisol is necessary for everyday function, it is the high quantity and prolonged duration of cortisol that can be damaging to the developing brain.

- **Plasticity:** Like playdough or clay, the brain is moldable throughout the life span. The brain has the capacity to alter previous patterns of communication. The brain is very "plastic" or moldable early in life, but this enhanced plasticity can be detrimental if the brain is exposed to extremely adverse conditions. The brain is both easily adaptable and extremely vulnerable during early life.

in neural connections is occurring while children learn complex skills such as walking, talking, reading, and writing. This period of synaptogenesis is a window of opportunity in which young children's brains are flexible and constantly changing. It is during these early years that the primary foundations of children's brains are established (National Scientific Council on the Developing Child 2007).

Sensitive Periods

During this early period of growth and change of neural connections between cells in the brain, the brain is primed to learn certain types of information. These *sensitive periods* are the windows of opportunity for development of particular skills and abilities. During these periods, the brain is exceedingly sensitive to environmental input. Some sensitive periods are "expected" because the brain is set up to anticipate specific kinds of input during certain periods of development. For example, in the first few months of life, the visual system of a baby goes through amazing growth. Babies can see very little at birth, but the human brain is ready to receive and process visual information during those first few months. Conversely, if babies do not receive that visual stimulation and information due to uncorrected cataracts or other visual impairments, they will likely never have typical vision. In these cases, the brain was expecting certain types of visual information that it did not receive at a crucial point in the development of the visual system in the brain. Essentially, the visual pathways were laid down without all the information, resulting in partial or complete blindness (Restak 2001). That is why corrective surgeries are often performed very early in infants' lives to ensure typical visual development (National Research Council and Institute of Medicine 2000).

Interestingly, different systems in the brain have different sensitive periods. Though babies' visual systems develop very early in life, the sensitive period for language learning is more protracted throughout the first few years of life. Parts of the brain responsible for higher cognitive functions such as planning, decision making, and regulating emotions do not reach their full levels of neural connection until adolescence (National Research Council and Institute of Medicine 2000). These sensitive periods have far-reaching implications for education. You cannot teach children what their brains are not ready to learn. For example, trying to teach a one-year-old how to write is something that the motor coordination systems in the brain are not yet prepared to handle. Instead, providing opportunities for developing language skills through talking and reading with young children is much more developmentally appropriate and is likely to set children up for success in learning reading and writing skills later in life.

Pruning

Another crucial part of brain development that is tied to sensitive periods is the concept of neural pruning. Think of a beautiful garden. Maybe it's at your local park or nature conservatory, or maybe it's in your own backyard. Think about the vibrant growth of different kinds of plants and how the paths look. Now think about what would happen if the groundskeeper (or you!) didn't spend time carefully trimming, weeding, and pruning back the plants to ensure they remained healthy and vital. Eventually, if the dead parts of the plants were not effectively pruned away, the plant would become unhealthy and die, being choked by surrounding weeds. The process of neural pruning in the brain is similar.

You learned earlier that the brain is born with most of the neurons it will ever have. You might think more means better. But just like a garden where plants die away because there are too many plants vying for the same space, water, and nutrients, the brain does not operate at its peak efficiency with too many neurons. In fact, the brain goes through a long period of cell death and reorganization in early life. And that's a good thing. The process of pruning, in conjunction with sensitive periods and synaptogenesis, is the way the brain truly becomes an organized and efficient processor of information. These processes assist in laying down the foundational connections that the brain will depend on for the rest of life.

During synaptogenesis, the burst of neural connections that occurs early in life, neurons begin reaching out all over the place to make connections with any and every neuron around them. As you can imagine, the brain becomes a busy web of tangles and connections. Think about a place like New York City at rush hour. The sheer volume of cars and people make getting anywhere a very complicated process. Similarly, early in life, there are so many neurons and connections in the brain that it is highly inefficient at communicating. However, through the information that the brain receives from the surrounding environment, the neurons begin to organize themselves and become a more coordinated system. The process of neural pruning occurs as the brain learns which connections in the brain are useful and which are not (National Research Council and Institute of Medicine 2000).

There's an adage that describes this concept: "Neurons that fire together, wire together." Essentially, as the brain begins to process complex information from the environment, it creates efficient communication systems of neurons that "fire" or transmit signals to one another. As these neurons receive and transmit information to and from one another, the connections gain strength and "wire" together.

Think about the first time you started working at a job that required a long commute. Chances are you had a few different routes that you could take to get there. Maybe you could drive or take the train; maybe you could take the highway or the side roads. The first few times you went to your job, you may have tried out different commuting options to see which was most efficient at getting you there on time with the least amount of hassle. After a while, you could easily determine which routes were the quickest and most efficient, and chances are they became your default way of getting to work. You probably didn't even have to think about it anymore because it became so automatic.

You can think about neural pruning in a similar way. There are probably thousands of different ways for a signal from one part of the brain to get to another part of the brain to communicate a message. However, over time, with practice and repetition, the brain learns the most efficient and effective ways to transmit messages across the brain and strengthens those paths. While that is happening, the other, less used connections are pruned away, making room for the stronger, more efficient connections to survive and thrive. Much of neural pruning happens in conjunction with various sensitive periods in development (National Research Council and Institute of Medicine 2000).

SERVE-AND-RETURN IN THE BRAIN

Building relationships with caregivers is one of the most important processes early in life. These relationships set up the brain for everything that follows. From the first days of life, infants begin interacting with the world around them and begin to build attachment relationships with their primary caregivers. Even in the earliest hours of life, the seemingly insignificant interactions between babies and their caregivers begin to set the stage for all subsequent growth and development.

As discussed in chapter 1, babies are born expecting and seeking relationships with caregivers. In fact, scientific research has found continual evidence that relationships are the "active ingredient" in human development (National Scientific Council on the Developing Child 2004b). These relationships not only provide stability and comfort for the infant, but they also provide the brain with important information about patterns and expectations from the surrounding environment.

Think about the process of baking a cake. You mix all the ingredients together, place them in a cake pan, and stick the pan in the oven. When you pull out your cake, you notice that it has fallen in the middle and did not rise properly. You then realize that you inadvertently forgot the baking powder, the active ingredient in cake batter that is necessary for your cake to rise properly. Similarly, relationships serve as that active ingredient in our development. In secure relationships with responsive caregivers, babies learn to anticipate and expect that their needs will be met. They expect safety and security in the presence of their caregiver. They anticipate being able to actively engage with the caregiver in learning and exploration.

Researchers have also found that there are certain brain chemicals and hormones that contribute and react to these relationships. Not only do caregivers provide exposure to sights and sounds necessary for the brain to learn, but research also indicates that when babies are in positive interactions with their caregivers, their bodies release hormones and chemicals related to positive emotions. Soon babies begin to associate the presence and responsiveness of their caregivers with positive feelings (National Scientific Council on the Developing Child 2004a).

These positive associations are built through the seemingly insignificant serve-and-return interactions discussed in chapter 1. Within the tennis match of interaction, babies will coo or cry out to their caregivers. When the caregivers respond to their needs or engage with them in chatter or babble, babies experience the release of positive hormones and chemicals in the body (National Research Council and Institute of Medicine 2000; National Scientific Council on the Developing Child 2004a). Conversely, when babies are upset or uncomfortable, their bodies release stress hormones and chemicals. However, the presence of a responsive caregiver can assist in stemming the tide of negative feelings and the physiological experience of stress.

WHEN SERVE-AND-RETURN GOES WRONG

When babies are not in secure relationships with primary caregivers who are responsive to their needs, disruption to brain development may occur (National Scientific Council on the Developing Child 2009). Without the active ingredient of responsive caregiving, the babies may not associate positive feelings of safety and security with their caregivers. Babies with caregivers who are less responsive may experience fewer engaging and positive interactions with the caregivers. These early responsive interactions are important for later learning. For example, research indicates that early word exposure may be linked to later reading comprehension and vocabulary. When caregivers use more extensive vocabularies when talking with their young children, these children tend to exhibit higher reading and vocabulary proficiency later in life (National Research Council and Institute of Medicine 2000). Children with less responsive caregivers are also likely to have more difficulty developing positive relationships with peers later in life (National Scientific Council on the Developing Child 2004b).

Maternal Depression

The detrimental effects of a disrupted serve-and-return relationship has been most often studied in the context of maternal depression. Maternal depression, including postpartum depression, is concerning not only because of the severity of its potential effects on the social, emotional, and brain development of infants, but also because of its prevalence. It is estimated that 10 to 20 percent of mothers will at some point in their lives suffer from depression. Furthermore, a mother's major depression affects approximately one in eleven babies during the first year of life (National Scientific Council on the Developing Child 2009). This is especially problematic because of the crucial importance of the first year of life in developing positive attachments and building strong foundations for brain development.

In the case of maternal depression, there are two primary types of parenting patterns that may result that are potentially destructive. One is called *hostile and intrusive* and exists when the parent may "serve" in a way that's difficult for the infant to "return." For example, instead of appropriately responding to a baby's giggle with a measured smile and laugh of her own, a caregiver may thrust her face abrasively toward the baby and laugh loudly, causing increased distress in the baby. It's like when young children are afraid of the clowns at the circus. Usually, children are fearful of clowns because of their strange makeup and over-the-top expressions and actions. Often this exuberance can be overstimulating for young children, causing distress instead of joy. This is similar to the case of the mother who exhibits hostile and intrusive interactions. This intrusive and abrasive behavior on the part of the mother can cause the infant to withdraw and avoid contact (National Scientific Council on the Developing Child 2009).

The other pattern, called *disengaged or withdrawn,* is when a caregiver does not respond at all to the baby's "serve." For example, pretend you have a problem at work, and you call a friend to vent and seek counsel on what to do about the situation. Your friend does not pick up her phone, so you leave a message to call you back as soon as she can. A day goes by and you don't hear from her, so you try to call again and have to leave another message. For the next three days, you continue to reach out to your friend with increasing urgency, but she continues to ignore you. Eventually, you give up trying to contact her, and because of her lack of response, you won't try to call her again in the future. This is what it's like for a baby who has a mother who's depressed and expressing a disengaged or withdrawn pattern of behavior. The baby tries repeatedly to get a response from the caregiver, with increasing distress, but to no avail, and eventually the baby gives up and become listless and disengaged (National Scientific Council on the Developing Child 2009).

Interestingly, not only do babies with depressed mothers tend to disengage from social encounters, but they may also begin to have brain activity patterns that resemble depressed adults (National Scientific Council on the Developing Child 2009). Furthermore, as with maternal stress during pregnancy, research has found that if mothers are depressed early in their children's lives, those children tend to show abnormal stress responses and raised levels of stress hormones later in life (National Scientific Council on the Developing Child 2009). Maternal depression can have long-lasting effects not only on children's social and emotional development but also on the development of their brains. But it's important to understand that maternal depression is not the mother's fault. Encouraging caregivers to find ways to access help and treatment when they struggle with depression is beneficial to both mother and child.

Stress and the Brain

Understanding what is meant by *stress* in the context of child development is essential. Scientific researchers have begun to describe stress in three categories: positive stress, tolerable stress, and toxic stress. Positive stress is the kind of stress that most of us think of when we say things like "I'm so stressed out!" Positive stress involves moderate, short-lived experiences of stress that are manageable and fleeting. These experiences are a normal and important part of life. *Positive stress* includes the feelings you might have when you're about to give a presentation to a room full of people or when you're about to get a shot at the doctor's office. While experiencing positive stress, you might feel an increase in heart rate or a rush of adrenaline. These experiences will be coupled with a rise in the body's stress hormone levels. These types of stress experiences are usually fleeting, and young children can learn to control their responses to these occurrences when buffered by the relationship of caring and responsive adults (National Scientific Council on the Developing Child 2014).

Tolerable stress includes experiences that are more intense than examples of positive stress and can be detrimental to the developing brain. Tolerable stress experiences might include the death of a family member or the loss of a home in a fire. These experiences cause disruption and emotional upheaval along with increases in the body's stress hormone response, but they tend to be time limited. With the presence of a solid social support system, children and adults can recover from these types of experiences (National Scientific Council on the Developing Child 2014).

Toxic stress is considerably more problematic due to its chronic and intense nature. Toxic stress involves strong, prolonged, and frequent activation of the body's stress systems due to situations such as chronic homelessness, abuse from a caregiver, or extreme poverty. It is the chronic nature of toxic stress that is most problematic, for it causes the stress system to be intensely activated for a prolonged period of time. Some scientists liken toxic stress to revving the engine in your car for hours every day, which can damage the engine. Toxic stress can have similarly damaging effects on the developing brain (National Scientific Council on the Developing Child 2014).

Biology of Stress

When people experience stress, their bodies release a variety of hormones, including adrenaline and cortisol. Both adrenaline and cortisol are crucial in everyday life because they help the body and brain cope with potentially threatening situations (National Scientific Council on the Developing Child 2014). The role of adrenaline is to increase heart rate, attention, vigilance, and blood flow to muscles during periods of stress. You likely think of adrenaline in connection to the energy or anxiety you feel when you're about to speak in front of an audience or get a shot at the doctor's office. However, the stress system also releases cortisol to help the body "gear up" to handle a threatening situation and maintain a state of high alert and efficiency. Cortisol's role is to suppress the immune system and reproductive hormones, but it also affects emotion and memory systems in the brain (National Research Council and Institute of Medicine 2000). By suppressing these systems, cortisol is readying the body to fight or flee from a threat. However, if activated frequently or for prolonged periods of times, cortisol can damage the body and brain.

In studying rats' stress responses, scientists have learned that sustained stress can result in impairments to memory, learning, and the ability to regulate stress responses (National Research Council and Institute of Medicine 2000). Evidence also suggests that prolonged stress responses early in life can change how some genes responsible for diverse aspects of brain function may be expressed, or "dimmed," impacting the development of brain cells and their functions (National Scientific Council on the Developing Child 2014). Furthermore, research has found that prolonged experiences of stress early in life can lead to increased risk for lasting health problems later in life.

Early in life, young children's bodies are beginning to establish lasting patterns that may influence their bodies' responses for the rest of their lives. In the case of toxic stress, the body learns that expecting constant threat is important to survival. Children who experience toxic stress tend to be more hypervigilant, as if expecting or anticipating threatening situations as a normal part of their lives. Their stress response systems adapt to the expectation of consistent threat, which may have a lasting effect on brain structure and function as well as behavior (National Scientific Council on the Developing Child 2014).

However, interactions with caring, responsive caregivers can play a vital role in stemming the tide of toxic stress and reducing its negative effects on brain and behavior. Confidence in the consistent presence and support of a caregiver helps lessen children's biological response to stressful experiences, not just their behavioral reactions. Furthermore, research indicates that even when children are overanxious or fearful, the presence of a strong, caring relationship with an adult can help to calm and buffer against the heightened stress response, thus lessening its impact (National Scientific Council on the Developing Child 2014).

Conversely, insecure attachments have been found to have detrimental effects on already heightened stress responses. Children who express insecure attachment styles have been found to have baseline cortisol levels that are much higher than in children who have secure attachment relationships, even when they are not frightened or under threat. Even at a low level of threat, their stress system is more active than children with more secure attachment patterns (National Scientific Council on the Developing Child 2014). Given what research has found about the potentially damaging effects of prolonged activation of stress systems on the brain and behavior, it is important to consider the power of these early attachment relationships on later health and development.

The effects of toxic stress, as well as a discussion about a few of the primary causes of toxic stress in the lives of young children, will be discussed at length in chapters 3, 4, and 5. For now, however, recognize that the brain is remarkably moldable and adaptable, despite the potentially long-lasting effects of early toxic stress. Plasticity is the brain's way of flexibly adapting to changing situations. Through plasticity, the brain can repair damage, learn new patterns, and form new connections.

PLASTICITY: BUILDING STRONG FOUNDATIONS

Early in life, the human brain is especially malleable, like plastic. There is evidence for brain plasticity across the life span, but the brain is never more changeable than in the first few years of life. This can be a double-edged sword. The first few years of life are the time of both greatest risk and greatest reward in brain development. To be sure, it's easier and more efficient to design and build the brain well the first time than it is to repair difficulties later. However, when working with young children who have experienced chronic stress, it is important to remember that plasticity offers promise of recovery from early adversity.

This type of turnaround from despair to hope was never more clearly seen than in the research on children raised in institutional orphanages. In parts of Eastern Europe, there was a period when orphanages were plentiful and care was meager. In many of these orphanages, infants and young children were exposed to horrific conditions of deprivation. Children were piled in cribs and left to their own devices day in and day out. They had very few, if any, relationships with caring caregivers and little environmental stimulation. With minimal contact from adult caregivers and poor food and medical care, many of these children experienced detrimental consequences of this early deprivation later in their lives (National Research Council and Institute of Medicine 2000).

In the early 1990s, when the communist regimes that supported such orphanages fell, orphaned children began to be adopted in the United States and Great Britain. Researchers later found that the children who were born into situations of horrendous deprivation but were later adopted into caring, loving homes often experienced substantial improvement in outcomes. In fact, children who were adopted into secure homes very early in life (before about one year of age) were found to show behavioral, cognitive, and social functioning fairly typical of their peers born into stable homes (Gunnar 2001; National Research Council and Institute of Medicine 2000). In other words, through positive interactions with supportive caregivers and exposure to more typical environments, these children were able to regain much of what was lost during those early months of deprivation. The plasticity of the human brain allowed for some reconstruction of brain connections and integration of new learning.

Yet children adopted later in their lives or into less supportive and nurturing environments often showed cognitive and social delays as well as increased occurrences of psychological disorders (Gunnar 2001). Though many of these children were able to regain some of their functioning and were certainly better off than children who were not adopted from the institutions, their adaptability to change was limited. In other words, the brain's plasticity in the early years begins to wane as time goes on, and making substantial changes to the brain becomes more challenging later in life. However, the presence of a stable and supportive caregiver early in these children's lives seems to be a primary factor in their ability to overcome extreme adversity. This evidence further underscores the crucial importance of supportive and nurturing caregivers in the lives of young children.

Resilience in Development

The recovery of many of these institutionalized children in the context of healthy, supportive environments is an example of a phenomenon called *resilience*. Resilience is the presence of positive outcomes despite exposure to threats or adversity (Masten 2014). Some researchers think of resilience

COMMON RISK AND PROTECTIVE FACTORS IN DEVELOPMENT

Common Risk Factors:

- poor health
- malnutrition
- poverty
- racism
- maltreatment (abuse, neglect)
- exposure to war, terrorism, or natural disaster

Common Protective Factors:

- positive, consistent relationships with caregivers
- positive relationships with other adults and/or peers
- self-regulation, problem-solving skills
- motivation
- faith and/or hope that life has purpose
- supportive schools, neighborhoods, communities

(MASTEN 2014)

as "ordinary magic." That is, that resilience arises from, and in the context of, ordinary processes (Masten 2014). For example, if John loses his mother to cancer but is able to recover and continue to be successful in school and with peers, he shows resilience in spite of his mother's death. Resilience does not mean John does not experience sadness at her loss or difficulties in maintaining his grades and connections with his friends. It is recovery to positive outcomes (good grades, sustaining friendships) despite exposure to adversity (his mother's death) that is the hallmark of resilience.

Resilience is not a trait that some people have while others do not. Indeed, someone who expresses resilience in one context (recovery from the death of a parent) may not be resilient in another context (recovery after a natural disaster). Whether someone expresses resilience is dependent on that person's access to protective factors (supportive relationships, access to good health care) in the face of risk factors (parental depression, a natural disaster). For people who have low exposure to extreme risk factors and good access to protective factors, resilience in the face of adversity is much more expected. For people who experience a high degree of risk in their daily lives and fewer protective factors, resilience to adversity becomes much more challenging (Masten 2014).

Yet what makes resilience so fascinating are the cases of people who, despite facing extreme adversity, are able to rise above the challenges they face and live successful, happy lives. Some of the protective factors identified above are at the core of that resilience. However, the necessary next step is understanding how people who work with children and families who face adversity can help promote these protective factors (Masten 2014). Children grow and learn in diverse contexts of families, care environments, communities, and cultures. Each of those contexts has risks and protective factors embedded in them. For care providers, identifying and promoting protective factors in those varied contexts is key to helping children to be resilient in the face of adversity.

CONCLUSIONS

Early in life, the brain has immense capacity for change. During that time, one of the most important active ingredients is being exposed to positive, nurturing relationships with caregivers. The relationships and environments that surround children every day affect how their brains grow, learn, and make connections. Early experiences can build strong or weak foundations for later development. The routine, everyday interactions between children and those who care for them are actually building a biological foundation and framework that children will carry with them throughout their lives. For more videos and other resources on how early experience builds the brain, go to my website (www.drlangworthy.com). As you care for young children every day, it is important to remember that you're helping to build the strong foundation children's brains need to be resilient, to survive, and to thrive.

LINGERING QUESTIONS

➤ **I've often heard people say that little kids don't remember anything from before they're three years old, so it doesn't matter what happens to them before that. Is that true?** No. What children experience before they are three is crucial. Though children may not be able to tell you about a memory from these early years, those experiences have a direct impact in how their brains are wired. The early experiences of children are instrumental in building strong foundations for later health and well-being.

➤ **So if kids experience toxic stress early in life, does that mean they'll definitely have trouble later on?** No. In fact, there is much research to suggest that even children who experience considerable adversity early in their lives can grow up to be healthy, happy adults. But exposure to protective factors like supportive and nurturing relationships is important for determining the likelihood of children expressing resilience to adversity.

➤ **I've heard that the window of opportunity for children's brain development closes after the third birthday. Is that true?** No. In fact, the brain grows and changes throughout life. As you are reading this book, your brain is changing! Though the early years are extremely important for setting a strong foundation and some sensitive periods for senses like vision and hearing occur primarily during that time, there are many other parts of brain development that occur throughout childhood, adolescence, and even into adulthood.

➤ **I use videos and music recordings that are supposed to boost babies' brains. Do they work?** There's no scientific evidence to support the idea that these types of media experiences help to build babies' brains. In fact, it's unlikely that any benefits that might exist would come close to being as beneficial as the important daily serve-and-return interactions between children and the people who care for them.

3 How What Surrounds Us Changes Us

No one is born fully-formed: it is through self-experience in the world that we become what we are.

PAULO FREIRE

CONTEXT IS EVERYTHING

As human beings, we are never truly "blank slates." There are people, places, and things that influence and change us throughout our lives. Even at conception, there are genetic and biological predispositions that affect who we are and who we have the potential to become. We are born into families, big and small, that determine how and what we learn about the world. From our earliest days, we experience the communities and neighborhoods that surround us and learn from growing up in those environments. Beyond our communities and neighborhoods are other influences, such as the states, territories, and nations in which we live. Our environments, and the people in them, teach us the life lessons that we will pass on to the next generation. It is this cycle of perpetual interactions that defines who we are, what we know, and what we can become. Thus, it is impossible to truly understand human development without considering the variety of contexts that influence our existence.

In the early days of psychology, scientists thought of babies as empty vessels ready to take in information from the surrounding world. This viewpoint implied all children were born with an equal ability to become anything, regardless of what characteristics were passed on from previous generations. However, scientists have begun to understand the complexities of the human genome and how it affects human life. The field of genetics has transformed the way that we understand how humans transfer characteristics across generations. Furthermore, the field of epigenetics, which explores the idea that the environment can influence how genes are expressed in humans, adds complexity to understanding how our lives are constructed from the very beginning of life (National Scientific Council on the Developing Child 2010). As discussed in chapter 2, a variety of biological and physiological factors take place during the prenatal period that have long-lasting implications for children and how they grow and learn. But biology is just one of the interwoven factors that may influence how children develop into adults. There are a variety of models for understanding these complex interactions. One of the more common models used in developmental psychology is the ecological model, developed by Urie Bronfenbrenner (1979).

CIRCLES OF INFLUENCE

As its name suggests, the ecological model describes how different parts of the human experience and surrounding environment interact with one another to influence the development of an individual. This model is also called the "circles of influence" model (see fig. 3-1). The center circle represents the individual child. Within the circle of the individual child are biological, genetic, and physiological processes that influence the child's capabilities for growth and learning. However, we also know that factors outside children influence how they grow and learn. Some of these circles of influence directly affect the child (relationships with family members), whereas other circles of influence affect a child more indirectly (parent's work environment).

The context that exerts the most influence on young children early in life is their relationships with people providing direct care (family members, child care providers). The family environment is a primary example of a context that directly influences young children's development. Because young children spend most of their time with their families, the structure and dynamics of families directly influence young children. Children learn through relationships with their caregivers, siblings, and other family members how their needs will be met within the family environment. Many young children must learn not only how to navigate relationships with primary caregivers but with siblings as well. Some families are larger than just the nuclear family (parents and their children) and include grandparents, aunts, uncles, and cousins. Other families include multiple households with step- or half siblings. All of these individual relationships influence what children learn about their surrounding environment.

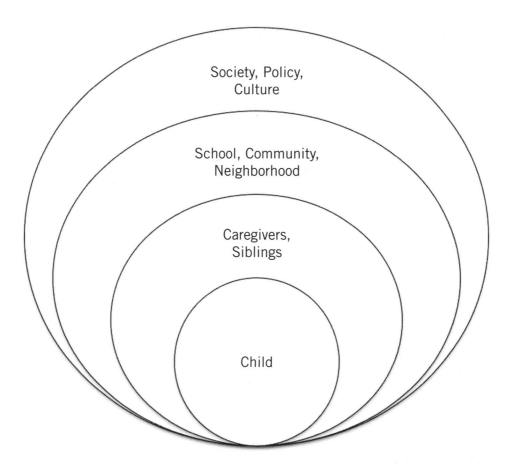

Figure 3.1. The ecological, or circles of influence, model: How different aspects of context affect development (Adapted from Bronfenbrenner's ecological model [Bronfenbrenner 1979]).

As previously discussed, children can learn to have very different relationships with different caregivers. This is important to remember as we consider the circles of influence that directly affect the child's growth and development. Not only do parents and family members have a direct influence, but child care providers, family friends, neighbors, and others who are regularly present in the child's life all have unique relationships with that single child. Yet the relationships between these people can also influence a child's development. If relationships between multiple care providers are in sync, the child learns to smoothly navigate between these different relationships. However, great discord between multiple care providers can create challenges for the child in navigating the relationships. For example, if a child care provider and parent disagree about appropriate discipline, that relationship tension may indirectly affect the child. The child may have difficulty navigating the different rules at home and at child care, and may pick up on the tension between the two adults. The relationship quality between people who have a direct connection with a child can influence how the child understands and operates in his surroundings.

Other circles of influence that more indirectly influence the child include things like school, community, neighborhood, and parents' work stress. These factors tend to influence a child more indirectly through their direct impact on the people who surround the child. For example, a parent's ability to find gainful employment may influence the parent's ability to provide food, shelter, and stability for his children. Lack of access to social services or educational opportunities can be additional stressors that families face. In addition, parental stress levels may consequently affect their ability to be responsive to their children's emotional needs. In addition, there are situations when these circles of influence may influence a child directly. For example, a child growing up in a high-crime neighborhood may witness acts of violence, which can be traumatic for young children. These environments can also influence the important people in young children's lives and, as a result, indirectly affect young children's development (Bronfenbrenner 1979).

Children are also influenced by the customs, policies, and cultures in which they live. Societal rules and customs influence the way we understand the world and how we act in it. For example, most people don't contemplate stealing their neighbor's car because they understand that this would be against the law. Such rules usually curb our otherwise selfish tendencies to take what we want for ourselves (especially if it's a really nice car!). We pass this type of understanding on to our children. Children learn what behaviors and actions are or are not acceptable based on family and societal guidelines. Furthermore, these large circles of influence exert their pull in other less direct ways. For example, the United States has policies that provide social services for communities needing assistance following a natural disaster. Without these policies, families might not receive adequate housing and nutrition and might not be able to reestablish themselves in the wake of a natural disaster. As a result, families could experience severe health and life consequences.

It is easy to see how broad-sweeping policies may have a direct or indirect influence on how families and children live. The contribution of culture adds another dimension of complexity and will be discussed later in this chapter.

OPPORTUNITY GAPS

It is not always clear how the circles of influence shape young lives. However, societal shifts, economic factors, and cultural influences all have the potential to affect the contexts in which children grow and learn. One recent example of the power of these external circles of influence is the economic downturn of 2008. Families across the globe felt the sweeping effects of this downturn. Increased unemployment rates meant many parents were out of work, suddenly unable to support or feed their families. Jobs became scarce and salaries remained low. Property values plummeted and left people owing more on their homes than their houses were worth. Foreclosures scarred entire neighborhoods, and families who were once financially stable were left scrambling to find shelter for their children. Government assistance programs became inundated with people needing services. As of the publication of this book, the United States is still trying to climb its way back, but it will likely be years before we see productivity levels anywhere near to those of the mid-2000s. The economic downturn caused a cascade of effects that had the potential to affect the health, education, and well-being of families and their young children.

Economic challenges can be a significant hardship, especially for young children. In 2012 the US federal poverty threshold was $23,364 for a family of four with two children, yet estimates indicate that a four-person family needs an income of twice that amount to meet basic needs. Furthermore, 25 percent of young children (birth to three years of age) live in families that are below the federal poverty threshold and an additional 23 percent live in families that are low income (below the estimated income required to meet basic needs). Note also that though European American children make up the largest percentage of children living in low-income households, young children who are ethnic minorities are disproportionately low income (Jiang, Ekono, and Skinner 2014). Extensive research indicates that economic hardship can contribute to a variety of additional adverse experiences, such as living in unsafe neighborhoods, experiencing hunger, or facing higher rates of emotional problems. In turn, these experiences can negatively affect young children's health, safety, education, and future well-being (American Psychological Association 2013; Shonkoff and Garner 2012).

A primary focus in recent years in early education has been addressing the achievement gap. The term *achievement gap* has been used frequently in policy and practice circles to discuss the gap in academic success between children who live in low-income households or are from minority populations and their more economically stable white peers. In general, children whose families have more financial security do significantly better in academic testing and have higher graduation rates than children who lack financial resources (Geoffroy et al. 2010). In addition, children from low-income or minority households tend to start kindergarten less prepared academically than their higher-income, nonminority peers (Haskins and Rouse 2005). These gaps become larger as children move through formal schooling. As a result, recent initiatives have focused on improving school readiness for young children as a way to decrease the achievement gap.

In more recent years, some professionals and policy makers have argued that the gap is not in achievement but in opportunity. That is, the gap in achievement is a result of a gap in opportunity to experiences and resources that promote academic achievement in the first place (National Opportunity to Learn Campaign 2011). Essentially, families who are struggling to provide for children's basic needs do not have the same access as economically stable families to resources that enhance school readiness in young children. This way of thinking about the achievement gap takes the focus off of individual children and their academic success and instead emphasizes the contexts in which children and families live that prevent access to opportunities that promote school success.

It is important not only to recognize gaps in opportunities but also to acknowledge family strengths. Despite facing adversity, most families have strengths that promote child well-being. Maybe a mother has to work two jobs to make ends meet, but Grandma can provide consistent and responsive care for a young child when Mom is away. Maybe a family lives in an unsafe neighborhood but is very connected to their church or community center where children can play and learn safely. These assets of caring relationships, community connection, and easy access to services are strengths that can promote positive experiences important for young children's learning and growth.

CASE EXAMPLE

Meet Jeanie and Derek

Consider the example of Jeanie and her four-year-old son, Derek. She is recently separated and as a result was forced to move into affordable housing in the city. Jeanie works two jobs to make ends meet. She works part-time during the day at a local community college as an administrative assistant and works as a waitress in the evenings. Despite having two jobs, she still struggles to provide for Derek. Sometimes Jeanie feels depressed and struggles to get out of bed. The family lives in a neighborhood with a high crime rate, so Jeanie doesn't often take Derek to the local park. However, on the weekends when she isn't working and feels up to it, she and Derek sometimes take the bus to the nearby community zoo.

Derek spends his weekdays at a local child care center and is very close with Ms. Laura, his favorite teacher. During the day, he gets to play with all kinds of toys he doesn't have at home and really enjoys story time. Sometimes his behaviors toward other children are out of control, but Ms. Laura is working with him on thinking about his feelings and actions. In the evenings when his mother is working, his aunt usually cares for him. He likes when his aunt watches him, because it means he gets to play with his three cousins who are all around his age.

Derek doesn't see his dad very often. When his dad does come to pick him up at home, his mom and dad usually fight, which makes Derek sad. Derek doesn't like going with his dad, because his dad's girlfriend's kids are mean to him. But sometimes he gets to see his grandma when he visits his dad. He likes it when his grandma visits, because they often bake cookies together.

Important questions to consider:

- What challenges does this family face?
- What are the family's strengths?

So often when we think about difficulties that children face, we are looking through the lens of identifying problems. Instead, it is helpful to begin with the assumption that every family is doing the best they can given the context in which they live. Each family is unique and has different strengths and challenges. Instead of focusing solely on fixing the problems, recognizing and promoting a family's strengths is key.

CULTURE AS A CONTEXT

One of the most often overlooked strengths of many families is their identification to culture. While there are many different definitions of the term, culture generally refers to shared beliefs, goals, and practices that may relate to race, ethnicity, and language (Howes 2010). In a report of the 2010 US census data, 37 percent of the population identified as being a racial or ethnic minority. By 2060, the number of individuals identifying as an ethnic minority is projected to jump to 57 percent (US Census Bureau 2012). This growth changes the landscape of workplaces, schools, and early childhood care environments and requires recognition of and respect for both the needs and the strengths of diverse cultures. Everyone has a culture, and many people identify with several cultures. Culture influences the way people think, talk, and act. As one of the most pervasive circles of influence on a family, culture permeates a child's experience beginning early in life. From spiritual practices, holidays, or coming-of-age celebrations to traditional foods, family structure, and language, culture affects every aspect of a child's life.

Currently, most of the primary perspectives on education and early care are rooted in European American cultural values. However, these cultural values, expectations, and environments are not the same across all cultures. Thus, many children are presented with a challenge of navigating very different cultural norms when they enter early care environments that are outside of their family's culture. Depending on the differences between cultures and the level of support children receive from people around them, navigating multiple cultures can be challenging (Kaiser and Rasminsky 2012). This can sometimes result in children exhibiting behavioral challenges in the classroom or in misunderstandings about children's intents or abilities. Research indicates that children who identify as nonwhite, especially children who

Protection (2013), by artist Mina Blyly-Strauss, highlights the "many structural forces that can be brought into play to offer support and protection to children and their families." For more on her work, visit: http://minasweebly.weebly.com/instructions-for-peace.html. Reproduced with permission from Mina Blyly-Strauss.

live in poor urban areas, are called on less frequently in the classroom, are criticized more, receive less praise, are disciplined more often, and are less encouraged to think for themselves than their white peers (Kaiser and Rasminsky 2012).

The primary culprits for these misunderstandings are worth discussing. A tension often exists between cultural perspectives on the role of an individual within the context of the larger culture. In some cultures, value is placed on individuals as unique people who should assert themselves and take initiative. In other cultures, the value of the group is emphasized, whereby individuals are extensions of the entire group and are responsible for being highly cooperative and in harmony with one another (Kaiser and Rasminsky 2012). These different perceptions of the role of the individual within the larger group present unique challenges in the early care environment. For example, in many early care environments it is common to expect children to assert themselves and demonstrate their learning. However, for children from more collectivist cultures that emphasize the group over the individual, asserting themselves in the way that is expected in the classroom may seem contradictory and unacceptable. Thus, children from collectivist backgrounds may remain tentative and quiet, trying to blend in with the group (Kaiser and Rasminsky 2012). Care providers may interpret these behaviors as indicators that children do not want to engage or are less intelligent than their more outspoken peers. This, in turn, may cause providers to engage less with children who are reserved, which may perpetuate children's silence even further.

Communication style is another common culprit in misunderstandings. Some cultures primarily communicate using what's called *low-context* communication, where words are highly valued and are the primary mode of communication. Other cultures place value on *high-context* communication, where body language and nonverbal cues are heavily used to communicate intent and meaning (Kaiser and Rasminsky 2012). For example, the common instruction to "use your words" may seem confusing for children from cultures where high-context communication is valued. These children may believe they are communicating perfectly clearly with their body language. Furthermore, the way in which language is used to communicate can influence how children learn and express knowledge. Often in early care environments, the focus may be on learning facts. For cultures where rational descriptions and rote memorization are expected, this is a straightforward way of learning. However, for some cultures where context is important to both understanding and conveying meaning, this way of thinking can be confusing (Kaiser and Rasminsky 2012). There may be the added strain of a language barrier. Care providers may interpret children's unsuccessful memorization or nonlinear thought processes as indicators of lower intelligence than that of their more verbally communicative peers.

Becoming culturally responsive to the children in your care is essential. Providing opportunities that reach a wide variety of learning styles is useful in promoting learning for children from different backgrounds. You could talk with parents and ask them how they handle children's behaviors at home. You could read about diverse cultural practices and think about how to infuse them more into your care environment. Perhaps you can spend time with a child to figure out what methods and strategies seem to be most productive for her. Above all, you can cultivate compassion and humility in your work with children from diverse cultural backgrounds and understand that there are many ways to care for each individual child.

Historical Trauma and Microaggressions

In addition to cultural differences in perspectives and communication styles, more complex historical factors may influence children's behaviors. When distinct cultures interact with one another, some integration of cultures is required. Anthropologist John Ogbu (1992) suggests that there are three primary categories that describe how minority groups integrate into a majority culture. The first category is *autonomous* minority groups (Jews, Mormons), who are minorities in number, but who generally experience many of the advantages of the majority society. The second category is *voluntary* or *immigrant* minorities, who come to the United States largely by choice, in search of new beginnings and a better life. These people, who still seek to retain some of their unique cultures, are likely to move smoothly into the predominant culture. The third category is *involuntary* minorities, or those who did not initially choose to integrate into the majority society. These groups experienced long histories of oppression, racism, and conquest and were forced into the majority society largely against their will. The two largest groups of involuntary minorities in the United States are African Americans, who are descendants of those who experienced slavery and oppression, and American Indians, whose ancestors were systematically relocated and massacred when Europeans spread across North America. People from these backgrounds may continue to grieve the oppression and loss of their own culture that resulted from slavery and conquest, and may perceive economic, educational, and social barriers as continued forms of oppression (Ogbu 1992).

Furthermore, research indicates that there may be intergenerational challenges rooted in historical events or experiences that have lasting effects on children and families today. Beginning with the study of World War II Holocaust survivors, Japanese internment survivors, and the descendants of those groups, researchers began to explore the long-term effects of large groups of people experiencing a collective traumatic experience. The term *historical trauma*, or *intergenerational trauma*, refers to a collective and complex experience of trauma shared by a group of people of common ethnicity or religion (Evans-Campbell 2008). The effects of historical trauma are expressed in people of those groups across generations through identifying emotionally with the suffering of their ancestors. Not only can the emotional suffering persist across generations, but the ramifications of historically traumatic events also linger.

One example from the American Indian community is the institutionalization of mandatory boarding schools of their children. In the mid-1800s, the federal government determined that American Indians needed to be educated and it mandated that children be sent long distances from their families to attend boarding schools. At these boarding schools, children were punished if they engaged in cultural practices. As a result of the systematic deculturization of American Indian children, an entire generation lost connection to their traditions, practices, and culture. This intentional act of cultural destruction has created deep emotional wounds and collective distress for many American Indian people today (Evans-Campbell 2008; Michaels, Rousseau, and Yang 2010).

People facing the effects of historical trauma may experience depression, worry, and anxiety. They may have a breakdown of cultural beliefs and values, experience substance abuse, and have significant health problems (Evans-Campbell 2008). When families struggle with substance abuse, mental illness, and health concerns, children may face persistent mental and physical health issues as well. It is through this cycle that historical trauma continues to affect people across generations.

In addition to experiencing the effects of historical trauma, people may also experience persistent racism in their everyday lives. Some researchers define these acts of persistent but covert racism as *microaggressions*. These are events that can occur regularly in everyday life and involve discrimination or hassles that are experienced by individuals from a minority group (Michaels, Rousseau, and Yang 2010; Sue et al. 2007). Researchers have identified three different levels of microaggressions. The most overt form is a microassault. *Microassaults* are racially explicit derogatory remarks or actions meant to cause harm to the intended person. This is the more traditional form of racism that is deliberate and conscious in nature (calling someone "colored" or wearing a swastika). *Microinvalidations,* in contrast, are communications that exclude or negate the thoughts, feelings, or experiences of an ethnic minority. Examples include a teacher repeatedly refusing to acknowledge students of color in the classroom, or a white person asking an American Indian if he is "really an Indian." *Microinsults* are communications that are rude or insensitive toward a person's ethnic heritage. An example of a microinsult is a student rolling his eyes when a classmate of color brings up a discussion about racial identity (Michaels, Rousseau, and Yang 2010; Sue et al. 2007). With microaggressions, the burden of whether to address the aggressive act falls to the person experiencing the microaggression (Does the student of color call out his peer for rolling his eyes?). As a result, individuals must navigate the added stress caused by persistent microaggressions.

It is clear that these types of microaggressions may easily seep into the early care environment, given that we are all a part of a broader society fraught with these microaggressive messages. It is worth noting that microaggressions are not by definition intentional. That is, a provider may unwittingly commit a microinvalidation by chastising a child for telling a story that lacks clarity and does not have a linear story line. In some high-context cultures, it is common for stories to be more circular in nature. In that type of storytelling, providing anecdotes and episodic experiences have more value than a clear linear story that has a beginning and an end (Kaiser and Rasminsky 2012). In correcting children for telling their stories in that way, care providers may unwittingly make the children feel as though their experiences of storytelling within their own cultures are somehow wrong or bad. Being aware of your own perceptions and cultural perspectives will help you work with children of different perspectives.

Cultural Humility

In recent years, the term *cultural competency* has become very prominent in the fields of health and education. Essentially, cultural competency calls for professionals to be aware of and understand different cultural beliefs and practices (Tervalon and Murray-García 1998). Though understanding different practices can certainly be beneficial and is an important step, there is a fine line between understanding and assuming. For example, if you have an American Indian girl in your care and you have spent a good deal of time reading up on traditional American Indian beliefs and practices, you may assume that she should behave in a certain way or that she has been raised to fit certain cultural norms. However, given the uniqueness of each individual child and family, it is important to fight the urge to assume that you know what that particular child has experienced or how she should act given what you have learned in your exploration of her culture.

Instead, the concept of *cultural humility* shifts the focus from the person receiving the care (in this case the young child) to the professional providing the care. Cultural humility begins by recognizing and examining our own cultural heritage, norms, practices, and beliefs. Then it requires understanding the ways in which our own culture affects the ways we see and interact with others. Cultural humility invites providers to think reflectively about their own biases and to be open to learning new ways of thinking and responding (Tervalon and Murray-García 1998). Along with being aware that each child has a unique cultural experience, being reflective about your own cultural perspectives may make it easier to effectively communicate with children from cultural backgrounds different from your own. Being reflective begins with recognizing and understanding our own cultural perspectives and values. Thinking about the ways that you have been taught is the beginning of the process. How did parents, friends, family, community, or society in general teach you to interact with others? Are you assertive? Are there strategies that you think are "normal" ways to react to particular situations? What is your ethnic background? How has your ethnic history contributed to defining your path in life and work? These are all questions that are worth exploring and contemplating as you approach interacting with children from other cultural backgrounds. Through this reflective work, you may find you have very specific perceptions about the world that influence you more than you realized. Keep in mind that this process is ongoing because culture changes constantly. Cultural humility involves becoming a lifelong learner. It requires a commitment to learning about yourself, as well as about people from cultures other than your own.

CONCLUSIONS

This chapter has explored some of the primary ways in which children's experiences with the world around them have an impact on how they grow and develop. Whether by direct interactions with family and friends, experiences in neighborhoods and communities, or the subtle but ever-present effects of society and culture, children experience a variety of contexts throughout their young lives. As care providers, we must consider those various contexts and the extent to which they help or hamper children's growth and development.

The next section of this book will explore what happens when young children are faced with extreme adversity in their early environments. Young children are susceptible to experiences of trauma and loss, and these experiences may have a direct impact on their development. The next chapters examine what we know about the effects of trauma and loss in early life, as well as how care providers can foster healthy relationships for children who have experienced trauma and loss.

LINGERING QUESTIONS

➤ **I try to incorporate various holidays into my teaching to acknowledge the cultural differences of the kids in my care. Is this enough?** This is a great start to being culturally responsive to the children in your care. However, culture is about a lot more than just holidays. Learning more about how children from cultures other than your own interact, learn, and behave can help you foster their unique strengths.

➤ **I can't control any of the experiences that children have outside of my care. Why do I need to know about their contexts?** True, you may not be able to do anything to directly influence the other contexts in which children live. However, being more knowledgeable about what children are experiencing outside of your care can help to inform the ways in which you work with them. In providing secure, responsive, and structured care environments where children can feel safe, you open doors for children's learning, even if other parts of their lives are chaotic.

➤ **How do I balance being responsive to children's cultural differences and maintaining high expectations for all children?** There is no easy answer. However, think about it this way: The expectations may not change (getting all children to learn the alphabet); it may be the process of meeting those expectations that requires some flexibility (learning stories to go with each letter versus learning the alphabet song). No child gets a free pass; everyone is expected to meet certain expectations based on his capabilities. But how you work with children to help them learn the skills they need to meet those standards may change depending on the needs of each individual child.

4 How What We Experience Shapes Us

It's wrong what they say about the past, I've learned, about how you can bury it. Because the past claws its way out.

KHALED HOSSEINI

Daniel came from an abusive, chaotic home. His mother was a drug addict with a long string of abusive boyfriends. Daniel often talked about how his mother would heat cocaine and use needles to shoot it or smoke it. As a seven-year-old, he was an expert in the uses and preparation of cocaine. Once he told me that he and his little brother hid under the bed while their mother was being beaten by her boyfriend.

When he revealed information that other teachers and I thought required intervention, we reported the situation to child protective services. Unfortunately, this backfired because they informed Daniel's mother that we had reported Daniel's situation. As a result, she took her anger out on him. One day, shortly after the encounter with child protection, I remember Daniel hiding behind me to avoid his mother when she came to pick him up. I learned from others in the community that Daniel and his younger brother would stay outside or at a friend's house until late at night. They obviously did not want to go home. Daniel's situation became even worse when his mother was paralyzed after passing out from drug use and being run over by a car. I later learned that Daniel's mother was continually beaten by her boyfriend, even when she was in a wheelchair.

In the classroom, Daniel struggled and became easily frustrated with difficult tasks. He would often act out and throw things, tip over his desk, and cry. Daniel did not interact well with his peers. He would often have a meltdown when he thought they were being unfair. Daniel would make growling sounds when he was under stress and could turn from being withdrawn to acting out in a moment. In general, his behaviors were somewhat episodic. He and other children in the town would have good days or bad days depending on whether their parents were partying heavily, which often coincided with welfare check distribution.

Daniel lived across the street from the school, and he could see his house from the playground. I remember one day Daniel was happily playing on the playground, and at one point, he glanced up toward his house to see a group of men carrying cases of beer into the house. After witnessing that, he became depressed and withdrawn.

Despite his struggles, Daniel was very good at working with younger children. His best reward was to earn time to be a tutor working with them. He made sure the children were comfortable and had everything they needed. Daniel had strengths in spite of his challenges, and I tried to deescalate his destructive behaviors and provide a safe environment for him to learn.

I was mostly kind and gentle with him as I tried to modify his behaviors. When his behavior was a danger to himself or others, I made sure he was in a safe place. On one occasion, I had to have another teacher assist me in moving him out of a very small computer room when he started kicking other students and the computers. We gently spoke to him and offered him reassurance to help calm him down. He became very attached to me and sometimes became jealous when I helped other students before I helped him. I was somewhat successful with him overall, but it was not an easy task. I also received help from the school counselor and principal when needed.

If I could go back in time and do things differently, I would change the "time-out area" to a more user-friendly setting, such as a "vacation area" for those who are under stress to take a needed vacation from the rest of the class. I would make it less of a punishment and more of a positive choice for deescalating and calming oneself. I think structure is very important for traumatized youth. I was a rather structured, somewhat strict teacher. I found children thrived in settings in which they felt safe and where adults provided structure. I often wonder what happened to Daniel. I suspect after he left my care his struggles continued, but I am hopeful that my work with him made some difference in his life.

—An educator's reflection

TRAUMA

Many children like Daniel experience early adversity in the form of abuse, neglect, and domestic violence with shocking regularity. These experiences are often called *trauma*. In general, trauma is the experience of an act or event that causes or threatens to cause physical or psychological injury. However, trauma is not just the experience of a threatening or harmful event, but also a person's resulting perception of the event as overwhelming (Michaels, Borsheim, and Lohrbach 2010). A traumatic event is characterized as having two components: (1) a person experiences or witnesses an event involving serious injury or death or a perceived threat to the self or to others, and (2) the person's response to the threatening event includes expressions of fear, helplessness, and/or horror (Hodas 2006). Some examples of experiences that might result in traumatic responses include natural disasters, abuse, neglect, witnessing violent acts, or the death of a loved one.

For decades, scientists and clinicians have studied the effects of trauma in adults. Traumatic events have been shown to have lasting effects on psychological functioning and often lead to post-traumatic stress disorder (PTSD). PTSD involves reexperiencing the traumatic event as if it is happening over and over again. People with PTSD often have experiences of being on high alert—or hyperarousal—to any perceived threat and may attempt to avoid or numb the emotional arousal associated with the traumatic event (De Young, Kenardy, and Cobham 2011). PTSD has been most often studied in adult populations, particularly in veterans and soldiers, and is often linked to other psychological problems such as depression and anxiety. However, researchers and clinicians have recently determined that PTSD can also affect young people. Research suggests PTSD can have a significant impact on the emotional, social, and cognitive functioning in adults and adolescents (De Young, Kenardy, and Cobham 2011).

Trauma includes chronic experiences of adversity and is not exclusive to experiencing a single traumatic event. For example, your house being hit by a tornado could constitute a single traumatic event. The event itself may be traumatic, but over time, the threat of psychological and physical harm passes. However, being in an abusive relationship where you are constantly at risk of physical or psychological harm would constitute a more chronic traumatic experience, because the risk for harm is ongoing. In some cases, multiple traumatic events (for example, abuse, homelessness, neglect, and domestic violence) are happening simultaneously. These multiple trauma experiences are referred to as *cumulative trauma* (Michaels, Borsheim, and Lohrbach 2010). PTSD-like traumatic responses can result from single events, from ongoing traumatic experiences, or from multiple traumas occurring simultaneously.

Despite children being at very high risk for experiencing trauma, scientists know relatively little about how exposure to trauma in infancy and early childhood is expressed emotionally and behaviorally (De Young, Kenardy, and Cobham 2011). Because young children do not have the ability to talk about their experiences and feelings in the same way as adults, it is often difficult to ascertain how trauma affects them. In addition, the *Diagnostic and Statistical Manual of Mental Disorders* (DSM-V), used to clinically diagnose disorders like PTSD, has very little information about symptoms in young children. Furthermore, a societal stigma comes with giving children a diagnosis early in life (De Young, Kenardy, and Cobham 2011).

Some people think children who are too young to remember the things that happen to them do not experience lasting consequences of those experiences. However, evidence shows that traumatic experiences early in life may put children at risk for emotional and mental health problems in adulthood (Michaels, Borsheim, and Lohrbach 2010). Even more troubling, emerging research suggests that children who experience trauma early in life can show symptoms of mental and emotional disorders within the first year of life (Lieberman et al. 2011). Furthermore, the well-known Adverse Childhood Experiences (ACE) study found that adults who reported experiencing trauma early in life (for example, abuse, domestic violence, parental substance abuse, parental incarceration) had greater health problems later in life. Specifically, people who experienced four or more of these adverse conditions early in life reported significantly greater health problems later (smoking, depression, sexually transmitted diseases, heart disease, obesity, and so on). In many instances, people reported experiencing multiple adverse events, and those who experienced cumulative trauma were also more likely to have multiple health difficulties later in life (Felitti et al. 1998). It is worth noting that the ACE study only accounts for remembered traumas. The high rate of traumas occurring before the age of three (see chapter 5, p. 89) should emphasize further that though children may not recollect or easily verbalize their early traumatic experiences, their bodies and brains bear the lasting effects.

Trauma and Toxic Stress

Trauma can cause major disruptions in the developing brain, specifically because of the body's response to threat and stress. As you may recall from chapter 2, when children experience threat, their stress systems are activated, and prolonged activation of the stress system (toxic stress) can cause lasting damage to brain development. Yet the terms *trauma* and *toxic stress* are not synonymous. Trauma generally refers to a response to a particular event or experience, whereas toxic stress is an internal state that results from the experience of trauma plus a child's inability to cope with that event (Michaels, Borsheim, and Lohrbach 2010). Essentially, a traumatic experience will most likely lead to stress reaction in the body. However, whether that stress response is toxic depends on other factors, such as whether the trauma is ongoing, the trauma is compounded by other influences, or the individual has social supports necessary for recovery.

For example, though the loss of a loved one could be considered a traumatic experience, the severity of the stress response will depend on other protective factors, such as social and emotional support from family and friends. With that support, a person may be resilient to the trauma and recover, experiencing a tolerable level of stress. Tolerable stress involves the activation of the stress system, but in the presence of caring relationships and protective factors, the body is able to regulate and recover successfully (National Scientific Council on the Developing Child 2014). When access to those supports and protective factors are limited, and other risk factors such as loss of a home or economic instability are present, a severer and more prolonged toxic stress response may occur.

We know from research that there are different types of experiences that can be traumatic to the individual (for example, abuse, neglect, serious medical illness) or to a larger family or community (for example, exposure to domestic or community violence, war, natural disasters) (Michaels, Borsheim, and

Lohrbach 2010). Regardless of cause, when experiencing a traumatic event, the body interprets the threat and initiates a stress response meant to promote survival under threat. This is a normal and adaptive function. However, if the threat is consistent or the fears of continuing harm are not allayed by the presence of positive and supportive caregivers, the stress system continues to be active.

Think of it like revving the engine of your car. When you are on the entrance ramp to the freeway, you need to press your foot down on the gas and rev the engine to get up to speed so you can merge onto the freeway. Once you have successfully merged, you take your foot off the gas, and the engine returns to a more typical state to maintain speed. Just as the car is meant to handle that revving of the engine, the human body is built to handle the normal revving up of the stress response. However, if you continued to press the gas pedal all the way to the floor and did not let the engine return to a more typical state, you would do damage to the engine, because the car is not built to handle that type of use over longer periods. Similarly, the human body is not built to handle intense, chronic stress.

Young children are especially vulnerable to the effects of stress not only because their brains are still developing but also because they lack the necessary coping skills and strategies. Instead, they rely on their caregivers to help them successfully cope with these experiences. In cases where young children have positive and secure attachments with caring adults, their responses to traumatic experiences will likely be lessened because they can seek help and comfort from their caregivers. As addressed in chapter 2, positive attachments with caregivers work as protective factors by buffering the child from stress and enabling them to be resilient to the traumatic experience. Conversely, in cases where children do not have access to secure, stable relationships, they may struggle to cope with the traumatic experience (Masten 2014).

Young children who have experienced trauma may consistently exhibit challenging behaviors. In an effort to cope, children who have experienced trauma may act out (hitting others, screaming profanities) or withdraw from others (refusing to be comforted by an adult, avoiding playing with peers). It's easy to see these challenging behaviors and become frustrated and jump to conclusions that children are behaving badly on purpose. Sometimes we can't help but think, "What's wrong with you?" when a child's challenging behaviors repeatedly tax our patience.

"What Is Wrong With You?" vs. "What Happened to You?"

I was recently reading a book by T. Michael Martin called *The End Games*, in which two brothers, Michael and Patrick, are on a journey. Throughout the story, the younger brother, Patrick, is on heavy anxiety medication because he sometimes "freaks" and becomes inconsolable and unresponsive. His behaviors are concerning and disruptive to those around him. At one point in the story, the brothers meet a man who sees Patrick's anxious behavior. The man asks:

> "What the hell's the matter with him?"
>   *Nothing is 'the matter with him,'* Michael thought defensively. *It's everything around him.* (Martin 2013, 104)

Michael's reaction to the man's question reminds us that we need to shift the way we think about behavior problems. Though we see behaviors as challenging or problematic, they are often merely expressions of inner turmoil. Later in *The End Games*, it is revealed that Patrick's anxious behaviors result from having an abusive stepfather. Michael's reflection reminds us that we must shift our questioning from "What's the matter with you that you're behaving this way?" to "What happened to you that you're behaving this way?" Instead of placing the blame on children for their actions, we must recognize the environments and experiences surrounding children that may contribute to their reckless behaviors.

BEING AN OBSERVING INTERVENER: THE EARLY CARE PROVIDER AS A SCIENTIST

Often care providers express concern that if they don't maintain strict control over a classroom, especially a classroom full of children who have behavioral challenges, their classrooms will become utterly chaotic (Koplow 2007). Though this concern is valid, teachers who develop skills of observing child behavior and recognizing triggers or potential issues before they become full-blown problems are often more successful in preventing chaos from ensuing. An observing intervener balances the tension between allowing children to create their own learning environments and experiences and establishing necessary boundaries for structure in the classroom. In some ways, this method of teaching is akin to being a scientist.

Before taking action, scientists do background research on the topics related to the overall question they want to answer. Scientists compile all the information they can find to come up with a clear idea of the scientific landscape before developing a line of inquiry. Similarly, teachers might try to learn about children's backgrounds, families, living situations, or previous experiences in a child care environment. This additional information about children can help inform how the teacher approaches providing care for them. Similarly, scientists use what they've learned to develop a reasoned hypothesis about the situation. Like teachers, who might try a few different ways of working with children and observe what works best, scientists experiment with these hypothesized solutions and measure their results. Just as teachers learn what works and what does not for particular children and adjust their approaches accordingly, scientists take results and use them to inform their future work and approaches to the situation. You might also think of this process in four steps:

1. **Background research:** Learning about each individual child. Just as a scientist does background research on a topic, you should get to know each child individually.

2. **Observing:** Moving from "I wonder" to "I expect." Early on in your observations you may think, "I wonder what this child will do in this situation." Over time, after you've observed him in a few different scenarios, you begin to think, "I expect that this child will act in this way."

3. **Experimentation:** Trying informed solutions and measuring results. When a child reacts negatively to something, you might try to redirect her to a new activity. If that doesn't work, you might move her away from the situation to have some quiet time with you.

4. **Progress:** Using what you learn to inform future work. Once you have a good idea of how the child will act in certain situations and what strategies work best with the child, you may find it much easier to minimize behavioral disruptions.

Children may react differently from day to day, week to week, and month to month in accordance with any number of contextual factors. You should consider what might be different about this particular occurrence of a behavior as you think through the following questions. It is important to be guided by your knowledge of the child's experiences and a variety of contexts:

- **Child's context:** What is this child going through? Does the child seem overstressed? Tired? Anxious?
- **Daily context:** What's different about today? Did something happen earlier that may have brought on this behavior?
- **Activity context:** What is it about this particular activity that may be triggering the child?
- **Peer context:** Are other children a factor? Have they somehow contributed to the escalation?
- **Your context:** How are you feeling? Are you emotionally capable of handling this situation, or do you need to find another adult to intervene?

Understanding your own context is as important as understanding the child's context. Your own feelings and actions may be more likely to determine the success or failure of your intervention than a child's feelings and actions. During the first months of a new year, or when there is a high level of child turnover, it can be especially challenging for providers to flexibly adapt to the new children in a room. During this period of learning and information gathering, things may be a little closer to chaos than providers may like, and more structure may be required to help children adjust to the new environment as well. However, research on this observing intervener type of approach indicates that it may contribute to less chaos overall later in the year (Howes and Ritchie 2002).

Though it is by no means essential to know exactly what young children have experienced in order to effectively work with them, it is helpful to shift the question from one of judgment to one of curiosity. Labeling children who act out in the early care environments as "bad kids" overlooks children's desperate attempts to cope in the face of trauma and stress (Gearity 2009). Instead, it is worthwhile to understand that children's early growth and learning may have been hijacked by persistent stress and trauma, causing them to act out in unusual ways to try to cope with their distress. Acknowledging that trauma may be at the root of children's challenging behaviors allows us to address the underlying issues causing the behaviors in a more informed and holistic way.

TRAUMA-INFORMED APPROACHES TO CARE

Recently, there have been shifts in many professional fields to provide trauma-informed or trauma-sensitive services and care for children and families. Trauma-informed care uses a purposeful and positive therapeutic approach to providing services to people exposed to trauma (Hodas 2006). At its core, trauma-informed care relies on providing an environment of physical and emotional safety for the person experiencing the trauma. In a trauma-informed approach, there is a deeper understanding of the potentially devastating effects of trauma and how it effectively changes the rules of the game of life (Hodas 2006). The focus shifts to understanding why an individual may be acting in a particular way, instead of just focusing on changing the behavior. With this understanding of the effects of trauma on human development, professionals may better understand an individual's triggers for certain types of emotional or behavioral reactions.

For example, if Juan's house burned down two months ago, Juan may become extremely agitated and act out when the local fire truck comes to do an educational day at school. Knowing that Juan may be having a traumatic response because of his previous experience can help the teacher effectively deal with Juan's actions. Instead of disciplining Juan for his unruly behavior, the teacher might take him to the corner of the room and talk with him soothingly and explain that he is safe in the classroom. This is an example of a trauma-informed approach to a child's behavior.

Recently, professionals have developed more systematic therapeutic

Building relationships with children through daily interactions helps strengthen their resilience to stress.

frameworks for working with children who express challenging behaviors that stem from traumatic experiences. Many of these frameworks recognize that children who have experienced early adversity are stuck in patterns built from their experiences of trauma and stress. These patterns cause behaviors that seem malicious but are, at their core, attempts to protect themselves from threats. Professionals can work to help children change their patterns and learn to more effectively regulate their behaviors in more positive ways (Gearity 2009).

Building Relationships to Build Resilience

Building relationships with children who have experienced early adversity takes place over time through consistent daily interactions. Just like the attachment relationships described in chapter 1, teacher-child attachment relationships develop through serve-and-return interactions. Developing the ability to control and flexibly adjust your serves and returns on the fly is crucial in successfully navigating potentially volatile situations with young children. As discussed in chapter 2, children who are stressed often lose control of their emotions and behaviors because their bodies respond to perceived threats of danger. The external expression of that internal stress state is often referred to as *arousal*. As with stress, when arousal becomes overwhelming in intensity, children lose control of their emotions and behaviors. Children respond by becoming dysregulated (not in control of their own behaviors) or by dissociating from the experience (attempting to separate from the threat) (Gearity 2009). Children struggle to learn when they experience high levels of arousal. Thus, the first job of a care provider must be to help calm them from their heightened state of arousal. This is done through providing connection throughout the turmoil and staying focused on their feelings instead of their actions when they are extremely aroused (Gearity 2009). By providing consistent and reliable patterns of comfort to young children, you are communicating that they are safe and secure in your presence.

Early on, children may refuse your help or comfort. They may withdraw from your offerings of comfort or actively push you away. These behaviors result when children have learned that adults can't be relied on to provide help and comfort when they experience distress (Gearity 2009; National Scientific Council on the Developing Child 2004b). Continuing to provide help, even when it is refused, helps children begin to understand that your presence and care for them are not dependent on their behavior. This may mean sitting quietly nearby when children are emotional and refusing your comfort. Your presence communicates that you will not leave them even when they are out of control. Eventually, many children will begin to recognize and even seek out your help when they are distressed and may begin to regularly use your presence to help curb their anxiety.

Once adults can effectively help children recover from their distress,

Tips for responding when children are highly aroused:

- Be a quiet, nearby presence. Sometimes even sensing that you are nearby can help communicate to children your willingness to comfort them.

- Use your words. The point of words when a child is highly aroused is not to explain the rules or to discipline, but instead to signal connection to the child's feelings ("I hear you, and I'm going to stay with you").

- Lower your tone of voice. This is not the time to raise your voice in anger or criticism. Raising your voice may signal further threat or danger, causing the child to become even more dysregulated. Using a firm but calm tone of voice helps children recognize that you are a stable and calming presence.

- Focus on the now. Instead of explanations of what rules were broken and how the child could do better next time, children who are dysregulated and aroused need the focus to be on their present emotional experience ("I see that you are not okay. I will stay here and keep you safe"). There will be time for learning and instruction once the child has calmed down.

(Gearity 2009)

children can then begin to learn how to think about and express their feelings in different ways. Because chronic trauma and adversity have disrupted typical developmental patterns, children who have experienced early adversity may not understand or be able to express their feelings very well. They may also seem to jump to hasty conclusions about others' actions, thoughts, or intents based on their own feelings. Incidents such as a peer accidentally knocking over a child's stack of blocks provide an opportunity to explain that another person's intent is not always hostile ("You thought she knocked over those blocks on purpose"). Then explaining that sometimes people make mistakes ("She didn't mean to knock the blocks over. It was an accident") can help the child begin to learn that the intentions of others are not always threatening (Gearity 2009; Koplow 2007).

You could also use these experiences as a way to help children understand and express their frustration or anger at the situation in an appropriate way. For children who have experienced trauma, emotions can be disorienting or confusing. Having had little assistance in regulating their emotions, and having experienced threats in environments that should be safe, children do not learn about the nuances of their emotions. Often young children do not have the vocabularies or the experience to help them discern between different types of feelings (frustrated versus mad; surprised versus scared) (Gearity 2009). Thus, providing children with the words to describe their feelings helps them begin to understand the difference between what various emotions feel like and how they can respond to those emotions ("You seem really upset at her for knocking over your blocks. It's okay to be mad, but it's not okay to throw the blocks at her because you're mad"). Through this process, children begin to understand that their emotions have ranges of intensity and appropriate reactions (Gearity 2009; Howes and Ritchie 2002).

One of the biggest challenges for care providers when working with children who have experienced trauma is to remain engaged while also being emotionally neutral. It takes a great deal of self-regulation to be genuinely empathetic while not letting your own reactions of horror or distress show. When children like Daniel tell the story of how he heard someone being beaten while he and his brother hid under the bed next to blood-splattered walls, it's extremely difficult not to feel sheer horror that a child witnessed something so disturbing. However, expressing that horror, either through facial expressions or emotional responses, can be detrimental rather than helpful for children. Though it may feel like the natural response to express your shock and mirror the child's feelings, empathy without distress or horror is the key. Children need honesty ("That must have been really scary"), but they also need care providers to be emotionally stable in order to feel safe and secure. If you are as emotionally upset as they are about the thing that happened to them, they are likely to become more upset and have even more difficulty calming down. Children are searching for stability and need someone else to be in control when they experience traumatic events like what Daniel experienced. Similarly, if you respond, "Oh, we don't talk about that" out of a desire to reduce your own anxiety, it communicates to children that they can't safely share their experiences.

Indeed, a natural response to something like what Daniel expressed might be "It's okay, don't worry." We mean this to express comfort, but instead it ignores children's feelings about their experiences and communicates that their feelings aren't important. Telling them, "It's okay, don't worry" when they do not feel okay may make them feel confused or ashamed that they feel worried. Instead, acknowledging how it must have felt for them is essential to establishing a safe and secure space for the children to explore their feelings and thoughts about the experience (Howes & Ritchie, 2002).

With consistent, positive interactions over time, children will learn to trust your presence rather than fear it. They will learn to use you to help them regulate their fear and distress. Once they trust you, it becomes possible

for you to help them begin to learn about understanding and controlling their emotions and behaviors. Through this process of developing positive relationships and helping children learn to regulate their emotions, you are building children's capacity for resilience to stress and adversity. It is likely that children who experience chronic trauma and adversity will require a great deal of time and attention in this process. The journey will be fraught with forward leaps and numerous backslides. However, through consistent interactions that meet each child's unique needs, you can begin to build stable relationships as a first step in fostering healing and resilience.

THE CASE OF JORDAN

Recognizing and Promoting Children's Strengths

Pretend you have a young child in your care named Jordan. You find it very difficult to work with Jordan. He is very boisterous, acts out constantly, is often disruptive, and frequently tries to get the other children to laugh at his behaviors.

1. Write down five strengths of the child in question. Dig deep and rethink some of the problem behaviors from a more positive frame:
   Deficits frame: Jordan is the class clown and acts out, disrupting circle time. He makes other children laugh and get off task. Strengths-based frame: Jordan has a great sense of humor and loves being with other children and making them laugh.

2. Look for those five strengths in the child every day. Make a mental note or write in a journal every time you see those strengths throughout the day:
   Maddie, a little girl in the class, has been very sad today because her goldfish died. Jordan made Maddie smile when he made silly faces. Then they played together for ten minutes, and you heard Jordan say silly things and make Maddie laugh. Afterward, Maddie wasn't so sad anymore.

3. Appreciate and praise the child's strengths when the child presents them in an appropriate way:
   During dramatic playtime, Jordan runs up to you and says, "Look at my goofy dance! Look at my goofy dance!" You might reply, "Jordan, your goofy dance looks really fun. Can you teach me to dance like that?"

STRENGTHS-BASED APPROACHES TO WORKING WITH CHILDREN EXPERIENCING TRAUMA

One of the biggest challenges in working with children who have experienced trauma and adversity is effectively recognizing and capitalizing on their strengths. The terms *trauma*, *adversity*, and *stress* all have negative connotations. It is often easy to identify the needs of children who face adversity and the behavior challenges they exhibit. What is more difficult, but equally necessary, is recognizing the strengths that can arise out of experiences of trauma and adversity.

4. Come up with one activity that you can do in the classroom to capitalize on those strengths so that you, other teachers, and other children can see them:

    You decide to play Simon Says, and you pick Jordan to help lead the first round of the game because you know he will be able to get the kids really excited and happy to play.

5. Establish and maintain structure in the classroom by reminding the child about when it's appropriate to behave in particular ways:

    During circle reading time, Jordan jumps up and begins his goofy dance, trying to make the other children laugh. You can remind him quickly, "Jordan, remember, now is not the time for the goofy dance. Right now we're reading together. Remind me at the end of the day, and you can show us your goofy dance before we all go home."

Though Jordan's behaviors may initially seem very disruptive, you may find there are creative ways to employ those behaviors in a way that positively contributes to the class and builds Jordan's self-esteem. In this way, Jordan's strengths are rewarded appropriately and he learns when it's okay to be silly and when he needs to sit still. But allowing for times and environments for Jordan to express his energy and exuberance safely and in a way that makes him feel good can teach Jordan that he has value instead of making him feel ashamed for acting out.

Fostering Children's Strengths

Thinking about children's strengths shifts our thinking about the child. Instead of passive, needy receivers of assistance, the children become resilient, active creators of their own lives. Shifting this perspective will also enable children to begin to understand themselves not as broken and in need of fixing but as contributors of unique gifts and skills. Think about the story of Daniel from the beginning of this chapter. See if you can identify not just his problems and challenges but also his strengths. What are his strengths? What are the positive protective factors that surround him? If Daniel were in your care, how might you capitalize on his strengths?

Maintaining focus on a child's strengths in the face of challenging behaviors can be especially hard. But recognizing and fostering these strengths can help us shift how we think about children who have experienced adversity, from identifying them as in need of fixing to seeing them as full of potential for resilience and thriving. A strengths-based focus, especially with children who have experienced adversity and trauma, will serve them better than the traditional deficit model (Hodas 2006).

Building Relationships with Families

Developing relationships with the children in your care is the first step toward addressing early life challenges. Because children grow up in the context of families, the various members of those families may play an integral role in children's development. Understanding the family context of each child is an important step to understanding children's everyday experiences. Establishing a relationship with the family to better understand the unique context of the child is useful in providing the most responsive and respectful care (Koplow 2007). Learning about children's family histories and past and current stressful challenges can be exceedingly helpful in understanding their behavior in the care environment.

Often one of the biggest challenges in working with children and families exposed to trauma is appreciating the family's competencies and strengths. It is easy to blame parents, especially in cases of abuse and neglect, for not protecting or providing safety for their children. However, understanding context is key. Children who act out may be behaving in a way that is adaptive given their experiences. Similarly, parents who are stressed or experiencing trauma of their own may act in ways that are seemingly irrational, but which may actually be adaptive in their particular context. Though we may assume that parents who are stressed "don't care about their kids" or "don't know how to parent," we ought to instead consider the possibility that parents are doing the best they can with the resources, capacity, and contexts that are available to them. Instead of focusing on what families "should have done," looking at the family's unique strengths and positive skills shifts the approach to children and families experiencing challenges. Viewing families through the lens of the "four Cs" (caring, competent, caught, change) is often a helpful way to shift your perspective from a deficit approach to a strengths approach. In essence, begin by assuming that, in general, families are *caring* and *competent* in many ways. Realize they may be currently *caught* in a situation that makes it hard for them to help their children. Then you can think about ways in which you could be a champion for *change* through your work with the family (Hodas 2006).

Furthermore, the act of merely recognizing and acknowledging the strengths you see within a family can be uplifting to caregivers and their children. For families facing adversity, the things they are doing well for their children (getting their children to child care on time every day for a week; affectionately greeting their children with a smile at the end of the day) are often ignored because their struggles are more outwardly apparent. Recognition and praise of those strengths can be especially meaningful for families and may help them begin to embrace their own competence and skills as caregivers.

CONCLUSIONS

This chapter presents basic information about trauma, how trauma and adversity may cause disruptive behaviors in young children, and some of the general trauma-informed strategies you can use to help build relationships with children. Through your consistent emotional responsiveness and stability children will begin to feel safe and be able to learn important lessons about their own emotions, thoughts, experiences, and behaviors. Remaining emotionally available while also providing consistency in structure is crucial to meeting these children's needs. It is also important to be mindful of children's and families' strengths and of other protective factors that can foster resilience to stress and trauma. For more resources on best practices for working with children experiencing trauma, visit my website (www.drlangworthy.com).

Knowing what types of trauma children have experienced is not essential to work effectively with them. You are instead working to curb the emotionality and behavioral challenges that present themselves as a result of early adversity or trauma. However, understanding some of the unique experiences related to different types of trauma, as well as the nuances of how children generally respond to these traumas, may help you better recognize and respond to children's behaviors. To that end, the next two chapters are devoted to the research and reality of some common forms of trauma and loss.

LINGERING QUESTIONS

➤ **Despite my best attempts, I have a great deal of difficulty interacting with a child in my care when he acts out and becomes emotional. What should I do?** Sometimes there are children who, for whatever reason, you have difficulty connecting with, and that's okay. If another provider is working with you, she may have a better relationship with this child and may be a better person to intervene when he acts out. If that's not an option, you may need to adjust your own behavior in working with the child to see if you can get a different response. Getting advice and help from other professionals can also be beneficial.

➤ **I feel pressured to focus on early academic skills in order to meet standards, but the children in my care (many of whom have experienced trauma or loss) are struggling. What should I do?** In many ways, the push for academics earlier and earlier has become increasingly challenging. We know that for young children, building strong relationships is a major precursor to later learning and development. Without those relationships, children struggle to learn how to control their emotions and behaviors, and subsequently have difficulties in school. Thus, the focus early in life should be on building relationships and teaching children to learn how to control their emotions and their behaviors. The skills they learn through the process of navigating the relationship-laden world early in life will serve them well in school and beyond. Explaining that building relationships can help to build language, self-regulation, and positive social interaction skills can be useful when you feel pressure to focus solely on standards-based learning.

➤ **How do I know if I'm building a strong and secure relationship with a child?** Chances are this will probably be apparent. But children with whom you have strong relationships will most likely seek you out when they are hurt or sad, respond well to your instruction and guidance, and look to you for help when stuck on a problem. In other words, don't overthink it. You probably naturally build these types of relationships with most children in your care.

PART 2

Research and Response: What We Know, What We See, and What We Can Do

Anything that's human is mentionable, and anything that is mentionable can be more manageable. When we can talk about our feelings, they become less overwhelming, less upsetting, and less scary. The people we trust with that important talk can help us know that we are not alone.

FRED ROGERS

5 When Those Who Love Us Hurt Us

The marks humans leave are too often scars.

JOHN GREEN

 "Ms. Linda! Ms. Linda! Guess what?" Demelza bounds up to me, bright-eyed and eager, the first child off the bus. The snow on her bright pink boots is already beginning to melt into puddles on the floor.

"What is it, Demelza?" I say, smiling, leaning down so my face is even with hers. I notice the bruise on her face is almost gone and her hair is newly braided. I could swear the bushy, green sweater under her jacket is brand-new.

"We're gonna have family night tonight!" Demelza says excitedly. "Mommy and Daddy are gonna be there. They said we are having a special visitor too. We're gonna make hot chocolate and watch a movie. If I'm extra good, then I get to pick it!" Demelza beams at me, clearly eagerly awaiting my excited response.

"Oh, wow! That sounds like fun!" all the while coaching my expression into the smile that Demelza expects, needs. I stand back up and guide the excited Demelza to her cubby to put away her boots and jacket. My eyes connect with Marla, my coteacher in the room. I know my eyes say what I cannot, and Marla nods, a tempered but frustrated look on her face.

It was not quite three weeks ago that Demelza had come into the classroom with welts on her back and arms. When I had asked her about where she got them, Demelza looked at me, her face ashamed, downturned. I barely made out her small voice as she told me, "My daddy bumped me and I fell down the stairs." She paused, and then added almost as an afterthought, "He said he didn't mean it."

"Oh, that must have hurt!" I exclaimed, barely able to contain my own emotional reaction to this news. "Did you go see the doctor?"

"No. Daddy said I'd get better all by myself. But my arm hurts." Demelza held up her arm to show me. There were angry red welts on her upper arm, and her wrist was swollen. I suspected a sprain.

"I bet it does. Here, let's go see Nurse Amy, and she'll make your arm feel better." I guided Demelza down to the nurse's office, while my thoughts were already on the impending Child Protective Services report I would have to file. This isn't the first time, or the last, I suspected.

Now I look down at Demelza, who is tugging at her pink boots, her excitement palpable. Procedure for cases like this is for a home visitor to schedule a home visit, which the family then plans for, like Demelza's family has done with movie night. This isn't uncommon when we report an incident to Child Protective Services. The home visitor will note that everything seems fine, there is not evidence of an unsafe home, and nothing will be pursued. I know the pattern well. I feel my heart rate quicken and my frustration begin to seep onto my face. I tamp down the feeling, quickly, knowing that my anger at the situation will do nothing to help Demelza now.

The squeak of Demelza's boots on the wet floor is what breaks my reverie. With one last tug she breaks free of the mutinous boot, chucking it in her cubby. She stands and grabs my hand, leading me back toward the other children, eager to start her day.

After all, movie night awaits.

—*A care provider's story*

WHEN CAREGIVERS ARE SOURCES OF STRESS: MALTREATMENT

Unfortunately, stories like Demelza's are not uncommon. In fact, recently in Minnesota, a four-year-old boy died of injuries sustained from prolonged physical abuse at the hand of his mother. Despite repeated attempts on the part of care providers to report their concerns to child protective services, the state never intervened. As a result, this young boy died (Stahl 2014). In response, Minnesota's governor has created a task force to review child protection procedures in an effort to make sure this type of incident doesn't happen again. Though this young boy's story has gripped the state and raised attention to the issues about the procedures on reporting and intervening in child abuse and neglect cases, he is but one of many children who continuously suffer at the hands of their caregivers.

In fact, very young children are disproportionately at risk for experiencing severe abuse or neglect in their early years. In 2012 babies in their first year of life had the highest abuse victimization rate of 21.9 per 1,000 children. In addition, 70.3 percent of children who died as a result of abuse and neglect were under three years of age (US Department of Health and Human Services et al. 2012). It is especially problematic when the caregiver is the primary source of the traumatic threat, as in the case of physical abuse, sexual abuse, emotional abuse, or neglect, because the child cannot seek comfort from the caregiver (VanZomeren-Dohm et al. 2013). These traumatic threats are termed *maltreatment*. Eighty percent of child fatalities in 2012 were caused by one or both parents. Of reported cases of child maltreatment, 75 percent were cases of neglect, 18.3 percent were physical abuse, and 9.3 percent were sexual abuse (US Department of Health and Human Services et al. 2012). A variety of factors increase children's risk of experiencing maltreatment. According to the US Department of Health and Human Services (2012), 13 percent of maltreatment cases reported in 2012 involved children with disabilities. Other risk factors for maltreatment include exposure to domestic violence, parental drug and alcohol abuse, poverty, parental physical and mental health issues, and exposure to community violence (Lieberman et al. 2011; Sanchez and Pollak 2009).

It is important to remember that it is not just a single act of abuse or neglect that has long-lasting consequences for development. Though those unique traumatic experiences are problematic, being continuously involved in an abusive or neglectful relationship with a caregiver can cause prolonged exposure to toxic stress and, subsequently, major disruptions to growth and learning (Cicchetti 2013). Furthermore, though less frequent but severe acts of maltreatment are extremely detrimental to children, research has shown that more consistent but less severe maltreatment also has long-lasting effects on development (Sanchez and Pollak 2009). In other words, regardless of type, timing, or severity of maltreatment, all such acts negatively influence development. Yet there is hope, because through consistent relationships with caring adults, children can show resilience in the face of maltreatment. The next section describes the research on the effects of neglect and abuse, as well as potential ways to boost resilience to maltreatment in young children.

Research

Over the past few decades, substantial scientific research has examined how neglect and abuse can have lifelong effects on individuals. Through this research, we have begun to understand the nuances of prolonged stress on the developing brain and its effects on how children think and learn.

Neglect

The most common type of child maltreatment in the United States is neglect—75 percent of all reported child maltreatment cases in 2012 involved some aspect of neglect (US Department of Health and Human Services et al. 2012). Child neglect constitutes the deprivation or disruption of a child's basic interaction with caregivers. As discussed in chapter 1, the early serve-and-return relationships with caregivers are important for providing not only safety and security but also the stimulation necessary for typical development. The absence of these important interactions and experiences can lead to long-term negative health and behavior outcomes (National Scientific Council on the Developing Child 2012).

Different types of neglect vary in their severity. Children might experience physical neglect in the lack of adequate food, shelter, or supervision from an adult. They might endure psychological neglect, or the failure of caregivers to pay attention to children's emotional and social needs. Medical neglect involves lack of access to necessary health care and treatment when children are sick or injured. Educational neglect occurs when caregivers fail to meet children's formal educational needs (National Scientific Council on the Developing Child 2012). There are also different intensities of neglect: occasional inattention, chronic understimulation, and severe neglect (National Scientific Council on the Developing Child 2012).

Most children likely experience what is referred to as *occasional inattention* on the part of their caregivers. In essence, caregivers may occasionally miss opportunities to provide important interactions and experiences. For example, imagine a baby is playing quietly on the living room floor with a stuffed animal while the adult is on the phone. The baby squeals and holds up the stuffed animal, looking for the adult to respond. But instead of responding to the baby's bid for attention, the adult walks to the next room to finish the phone call in relative quiet. The baby may squeal repeatedly to try to get the caregiver's attention and become increasingly distressed because the caregiver still does not respond. After a few minutes, the adult ends the phone call and returns to the baby to provide comfort. If the act of ignoring the child's needs occurs infrequently within the context of an otherwise caring supportive environment, there are not likely to be negative consequences. In fact, some research indicates that occasional inattention on the part of caregivers may actually be an important part of the development of self-concept for young children (National Scientific Council on the Developing Child 2012). However, repeated instances of inattention of infants' basic needs are detrimental to development.

Chronic understimulation results when children regularly have a lack of important experiences necessary for building strong cognitive, social, and emotional skills. Perhaps caregivers provide very few opportunities for meaningful interaction with their children, or the children spend substantial and frequent periods of time in front of the television. This type of neglect often occurs because caregivers lack knowledge about the importance of the parent-child relationship in early life. Chronic understimulation may lead to less optimal cognitive, language, and social skills in children (National Scientific Council on the Developing Child 2012).

Severe neglect, or the persistent absence or disturbances of necessary interactions with caregivers, can result in disruptions in many necessary functions. Research with children from institutionalized settings has found that severe neglect can lead to abnormalities in both the structure and function in the developing brain (National Scientific Council on the Developing Child 2012). Many of the areas of the brain most at risk in such situations play crucial roles in learning, attention, thinking, controlling emotions, and regulating responses to stress. Additionally, neglect is linked to abnormal responses to stress in children. These disruptions may even lead to cardiovascular and immune system problems later in life. Some research has found that the effects of child neglect can be even more problematic than physical abuse, specifically with respect to cognitive delays. Children experiencing neglect have been shown to have lower IQ scores, lower academic success, and poorer language and reading skills than typically developing children (National Scientific Council on the Developing Child 2012).

Unlike children experiencing abuse, who are more likely to be hyper-aware of potentially negative emotions (see the next section for more details), children experiencing neglect have been shown to have difficulty discriminating between different types of emotions (Sanchez and Pollak 2009). In research studies, children who experienced neglect had a harder time discriminating between different types of emotional facial expressions than their peers who were not neglected. Furthermore, when children who have experienced neglect do successfully discriminate between emotions, they take longer and are less accurate than children who are not neglected (Sanchez and Pollak 2009). This may be due to a lack of experience with expressions and responses because of limited interaction with caregivers.

Neglect also plays a significant role in children's relationships. Children experiencing neglect show higher rates of insecure attachments to their care-givers. Interestingly, young children who experience neglect may be more likely to become too dependent on their child care providers. They may become very clingy or easily upset when the provider leaves or attempts to work with another child. Conversely, children who have been neglected may show limited social skills with other children, making it difficult to effectively engage in play with peers (Howes and Ritchie 2002). These children have also been shown to have higher rates of behavioral and emotional problems, even when compared to physically abused children (National Scientific Council on the Developing Child 2012). Because of these challenges, children who have been neglected can easily become outcasts in the early care environment. They can be especially challenging to work with, and large amounts of time and energy are required to coach children with histories of neglect on how to properly interact with care providers and peers (Howes and Ritchie 2002). Whereas children who have not experienced neglect have had a variety of experiences throughout their young lives that have allowed them to practice interacting with others, children who have been neglected have had less experience practicing those skills.

Abuse

Despite some overarching similarities, there are unique differences between the experiences and outcomes of children exposed to abuse versus those exposed to neglect. Though physical and sexual abuse cases receive more nationwide attention than child neglect, they are actually less common (US Department of Health and Human Services et al. 2012). Physical abuse is the most common form of maltreatment after neglect. Physical abuse is defined differently by different states, but in general it involves an act that results in physical injury to the child. Signs that a child has been physically abused include frequent physical injuries that do not fit the explanation by parent or child, consistent tardiness or absence from the care environment, and difficulties walking or moving. Children who have been physically abused may be reluctant to share about their abuse because of fear of caregiver retribution, fear of getting the caregiver in trouble, or a belief that it is acceptable for an adult to physically harm them (NCTSN 2009).

Sexual abuse, though the least documented of maltreatment types, is still a reality for some young children. Sexual abuse includes not only physical contact but also nonphysical acts such as voyeurism. Sexual predators often use manipulation as opposed to force, sometimes through buying children gifts or arranging special activities together (NCTSN 2007). Signs that children have experienced sexual abuse include withdrawn behavior, anxiety, depression, nightmares, angry outbursts, expressing inappropriate sexual themes in play, and not wanting to be left alone with specific people. Children may not report sexual abuse because of fear of retribution, feelings of shame or guilt, or fear of not being believed (NCTSN 2007). Furthermore, very young children may not have the language skills to successfully express their experience. Though physical and sexual abuse are different experiences, in the research literature they are often treated as subtypes of abuse. For the purposes of this section, the term *abuse* refers to both physical and sexual abuse experiences unless otherwise noted.

During the development of important attachment relationships early in life, abuse can have detrimental effects on children's learning and development. When the abuser is a parent or guardian (which is true in over 80 percent of cases of maltreatment), children lose confidence in their caregiver as a provider of safety and comfort. Researchers and practitioners often call this *complex trauma* because it occurs repeatedly within the context of the relationships children rely on for safety (NCTSN, n.d.-a). Children who have been abused are likely to develop insecure attachments with their caregivers. These insecure attachments, compounded by the trauma of being abused, make coping extremely difficult. This is especially true because young children are so dependent on adults around them to help them regulate their emotions and cope with stressful situations. When the caregiver is the cause and not the reliever of stress, children are left to their own devices to cope with their intense emotions.

In general, abuse leads to a high risk of physical and mental health issues later in life. Children who are victims of abuse often have delayed social and cognitive abilities and poor emotion recognition and regulation (Sanchez and Pollak 2009). They may also show more aggression and an increased tendency to withdraw during interactions with other children. Interestingly, research has shown that children who were physically abused are very good at differentiating angry facial expressions and show increases in brain activity when processing angry faces (Sanchez and Pollak 2009). Children who have experienced abuse have also been found to identify neutral facial expressions as angry (Sanchez and Pollak 2009). It is likely that children who have been abused have learned to become very quick to recognize anger in facial expressions so they can anticipate danger and protect themselves from being hurt. Recognizing angry faces quickly so as to avoid an abuse episode is beneficial, or adaptive, to survival and safety in the context of an abusive relationship.

In his novel *The End Games*, author T. Michael Martin describes this type of emotional hyperawareness through the eyes of his young protagonist:

> But soon . . . sometimes . . . [Ron] comes home at night feeling mean.
> And the kid learns to tread carefully, then, yes-yes. Learns to look into Ron's eyes and gauge the man's moods. Learns to walk into a room and instantaneously detect the emotional temperature. Learns to know how to act and speak to defuse Ron when the kid senses Ron's countdown ticking.
> Neat tricks. (Martin 2013, 117)

When this type of emotional hyperawareness is expressed in the early care environment, it can be disruptive and make for challenging peer interactions. For example, if a child interprets a care provider's face, voice, or body language as threatening, even if no threat or anger was intended, the child's stress system is activated because of the perceived threat. As a result, the child might freeze or run away from the provider. Alternatively, the child may lash out at the provider. It is important to remember in these interactions that the child is acting out of fear, not out of willful defiance. When children act out of pure instinct and their experience of the physiological fight or flight response, they are not able to think through and regulate their feelings on their own. They require help from adults (Gearity 2009; Howes and Ritchie 2002).

Apart from these potential emotional challenges, there are links between abuse and other difficult situations later in life. Children who have experienced abuse are more at risk for conduct and aggression problems, depression, substance abuse, and anxiety (Sanchez and Pollak 2009). Furthermore, because of the potential prolonged activation of the body's stress response system in cases of chronic abuse, children may be at higher risk for cardiovascular diseases, diabetes, and stroke later in life (National Scientific Council on the Developing Child 2014).

Despite these documented challenges facing children who are maltreated, there is also evidence that cognitive, social, behavioral, and emotional functioning may be regained if children are placed into safe, supportive, and caring environments. Evidence shows that some children who are maltreated may express resilience in spite of adversity (Cicchetti 2013). For children who face maltreatment, self-esteem, self-reliance, and self-confidence appear to be especially important characteristics in promoting resilience. For some children who have experienced maltreatment, reciprocal friendships, self-control, and active coping skills are especially predictive of later resilience (Cicchetti 2013).

Children experiencing severe neglect or abuse may require extensive counseling and interventions to regain skills and abilities (National Research Council and Institute of Medicine 2000). Indeed, the most successful models include intensive therapeutic interventions that involve the child and family. A couple of the more common interventions used for addressing maltreatment include Attachment and Biobehavioral Catch-Up (ABC) intervention and Child-Parent Psychotherapy (CPP). ABC intervention focuses on improving attachment relationships between children and their caregivers through increasing caregivers' sensitivity and responsiveness to the serve-and-return interactions with their young children. Research indicates that after ABC treatment, young children not only had more positive relationships with their caregivers, but also showed more typical patterns of stress responses (National Scientific Council on the Developing Child 2012). In CPP treatment, the focus of treatment is not solely on the child or the caregiver but on their relationship. Caregivers and their children participate in joint sessions with a therapist. Through integrating an understanding of the caregivers' surrounding context, recognizing their strengths, and increasing their understanding and capacity to be responsive to their children, CPP works to repair the trust between caregivers and children (Lieberman et al. 2011; National Scientific Council on the Developing Child 2012). This type of trauma-informed and relationship-focused therapy can help to rebuild the important relationship connections between caregivers and their children.

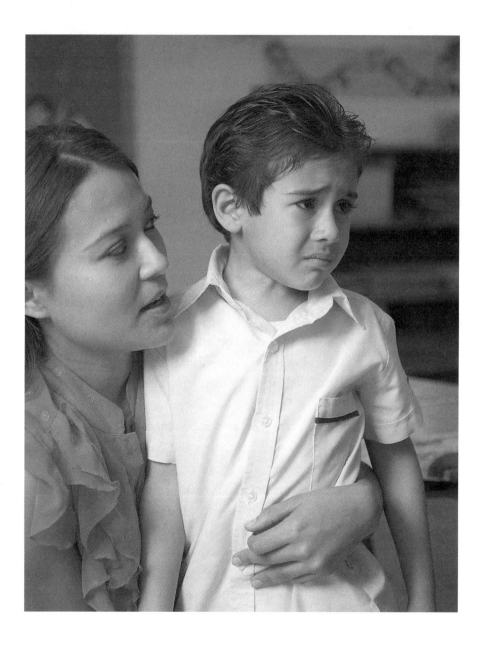

Response

Children who experience maltreatment also benefit from building relationships with other adults and practicing skills of self-regulation and coping. Children who experience abuse may act very differently than children who have experienced neglect.

Neglect

Children who experience neglect may seem to have little to no interest in other children or adults in the care environment. Their play may be simplistic and somewhat repetitive. Children who have experienced neglect may have a surprising knowledge of self-care activities, above and beyond other children in the care environment, because of their need to be able to take care of themselves—and possibly their siblings—without the help of a parent in the home environment (Koplow 2007). Children experiencing neglect may also engage in repetitive play that lacks the carefree and imaginative characteristics of other children's play. This is likely due to the lack of experience with play in a safe and supportive home environment.

Children who are experiencing neglect may be some of the more well-behaved and quiet children in the care environment. They may not interact much with peers, may withdraw from group play, may seem disengaged from the rest of the group, and may quietly obey instructions without outburst or complaint (Hodas 2006; Howes and Ritchie 2002; Koplow 2007). They may seem disengaged and ambivalent about their surroundings. In other words, they may seem like the "easy" children. However, sometimes "easy" can be a warning sign of deeper concerns. Children experiencing neglect are likely to express characteristics of insecure attachments, such as ambivalence about the presence of an adult. They may also seem very withdrawn and more likely to exhibit symptoms of depression (Hodas 2006). Because of their generally cooperative behavior, children experiencing neglect may be more under-identified than children who experience other types of trauma that result in acting-out behaviors. Because neglect is the most common form of child maltreatment, it is important to be vigilant and aware of not only the children who act out but also those who are quiet and withdrawn.

Spending time developing relationships with children who have experienced neglect helps them to grow and flourish. Such children may seem drawn to you or another adult, but then may become very frustrated or upset if you move to assist another child. They may seem to require your presence in order to behave appropriately. It can be useful to structure the care environment in a way that allows these children to feel safe and secure in your presence either by proximity (for example, asking them to sit close to you) or by providing structured and consistent interactions at the beginning and end of the day (for example, always walking them to their cubby at the end of the day, talking with them for a few minutes every morning when they arrive) (Howes and Ritchie 2002). Consistent and reliable interactions help children with histories of neglect build confidence in you as a care provider. Because they do not have a great deal of experience with supportive and caring relationships, they may act well below their chronological age and may require significant coaching and repeated interactions to get them to where they can more freely interact with other adults and children. They may need to be purposefully drawn into activities with other children and may require more encouragement and coaching on how to have meaningful interactions with playmates (Hodas 2006; Howes and Ritchie 2002).

Of course, not all children who have experienced neglect act in the same ways. Some may be more likely to seek out connection with adults indiscriminately—a phenomenon researchers call *indiscriminant friendliness*. In the case of indiscriminate friendliness, children may not have a strong connection with any particular adult, but instead are happy to be with anyone. Children who show indiscriminant friendliness toward strangers exhibit little to no "stranger danger." In addition, they may seem to get as much or more comfort from the presence of a stranger than the presence of a known adult. For children who seem to struggle with this, you might consider focusing on setting up some expectations when you know children are likely to meet strangers. You might require children to ask your permission before they talk with a stranger. You might also consider talking with children about the fact that all strangers may not be friendly, and that in order to stay safe it is important to tell an adult they know before talking with the stranger (University of Pittsburgh Office of Child Development, n.d.).

Abuse

Children who have experienced abuse may persistently act out in the care environment. They may have attention and self-regulation difficulties, experience altercations with other children or adults, and seem to intentionally seek out opportunities to cause disruption (Hodas 2006). A common feeling among professionals who work with behaviorally dysregulated children is that the children are intentionally acting out, or that they are trying to cause problems and manipulate adults through their behaviors. In reality, children act out not because they are in control, but because they are out of control. They are grasping for some semblance of order in their ever-chaotic lives. Their screams and curses come from the need for structure, stability, and guidance, not out of a thirst for power. In other words, children experiencing maltreatment act the way they do because they have learned in an ever-threatening environment when to observe, when to run, and when to fight. They have learned what will help them to survive in their unpredictably threatening environment. But when they try to use those same responses to navigate an unthreatening care environment, their behaviors may seem irrational and needlessly disruptive.

Though a care provider's natural response to a child's outburst might be to try to control the child's behaviors, children who act based on fear need to be able to express their emotions safely in the presence of a calm adult. Thus, focusing on soothing the child in the moment of fear ("I see from your body that you have big feelings" or "I'm going to stay right here with you") helps to bring a child back from her intense physiological response to threat (Gearity 2009).

Not only are children who have experienced abuse more sensitive to angry facial expressions, but they also tend to misunderstand certain emotional situations. Children who have been abused might consider anger or sadness as potentially appropriate emotional reactions to a positive situation (Sanchez and Pollak 2009). Sometimes it can be helpful to explain to children that smiling is okay when something good happens ("You can smile when I say 'you did a good job.' See how that feels"). This helps them to link positive expressions with good experiences and understand that when something good happens, it's okay to feel happy (Gearity 2009).

As a result of misreading emotional cues, they may miss other relevant pieces of information in a situation and jump to conclusions based on previous experience. For example, imagine Laia is playing nicely with blocks with Julie. Then Julie accidentally bumps Laia's tower and it topples over. Julie immediately apologizes for knocking over the blocks. Laia yells angrily at Julie for knocking her blocks over, saying, "You did it on purpose! You're mean!" causing Julie to become upset and tearful. Though Julie's intent was not to knock over Laia's blocks, Laia immediately jumps to the conclusion that Julie is trying to be mean to her and destroy her tower. As a result, Julie is reluctant to play with Laia again because Laia was angry and harsh with her for accidentally knocking down the blocks. This is an example of a child misunderstanding the emotional cues and attributing a hostile intent to an action that was not meant to be hurtful. In this example, Laia is very sensitive to other people's actions and has learned to expect that other people are intentionally trying to hurt her. These types of outbursts can have long-term implications for children when they are developing friendships with peers. If Laia is oversensitive and tends to overreact, other children are less likely to want to play with her. In addition, if Laia acts out in other ways in the care environment (speaking out of turn in circle time; getting irritable during transition from playtime to naptime; having difficulty controlling her movements and bumping into other children frequently), she may quickly become known as the "problem child." Laia may learn to internalize that label, while still being unable to control her behaviors. This may lead to Laia being often alone and lacking social connections with peers, which can increase her isolation in early and middle childhood.

However, it can be beneficial if you as a provider are able to approach children like Laia with an understanding that their behaviors are not driven by malice or ill will, but rather by survival instincts. Often this means pulling the emotion out of the situation by acknowledging any angry or sad feelings, and then once the child has calmed, focusing on the behavior itself. For example, in the case of Laia, saying something like, "Laia, it looks like you're angry. Your fingers are squeezed tight and your eyebrows are bunchy. It's okay to tell Julie you're angry. You can say, 'It makes me angry when you knock over my blocks.' But screaming at Julie is scary, and we want everyone to feel safe here. When you use your words at school, it helps everybody be safe." This effectively acknowledges that Laia is allowed to feel angry, but acting on that anger in a way that is frightening to others in the classroom is not allowed. Acknowledging children's feelings can be a powerful way to help them understand that they are cared for and safe. If their feelings are not acknowledged, but they are instead chastised ("Laia, you're being mean to Julie"), children may begin to feel shame and that they do not matter to the adults around them. Without that security of being with an adult who cares about them, their behaviors are not likely to improve. In fact, shaming or punitive discipline can exacerbate the behaviors, and in the worst case scenarios, lead to retraumatization of children (Hodas 2006).

To be clear, acknowledging children's feelings when they are acting out does not mean that the rules and structure of the environment should be compromised. Indeed, rules about safety and security must be maintained and upheld. The implementation of those rules may look a little different than in traditional methods. For example, instead of sending a child to the seat in the corner away from the group, consider having the child sit next to you until he is calmer and more collected. This way the child feels safe and may be able to reengage in activities more quickly. Instead of raising your voice at a child, use a calm but firm voice to explain the consequences of problem behaviors. Reminding children of the rules when enacting discipline is helpful as children may not always remember or know why something they did was wrong, especially if it is an observed behavior learned at home (Howes and Ritchie 2002; Koplow 2007).

Children who have experienced maltreatment may be delayed in language development, which typically undergoes growth spurts during early childhood. Thus, talking with children about their feelings and actions can be especially important to help them learn the words for what they are feeling. You might periodically talk with children about their behaviors to help them reflect on things that went well and things that did not go well. However, as discussed in chapter 4, you need to choose your moments carefully for talking through what happened. When children are emotionally and behaviorally out of control, they are not likely to understand behavioral instruction (Gearity 2009). Instead, dealing directly with the behavior, especially if it involves the safety of another child in the room, is imperative. Returning to discuss the incident with the child later in the day, when the child has had a chance to calm down, can help him learn how to understand behavior in a less emotional context. You could say something like, "Remember when you hit Tommy during circle time? Hitting is really scary. We don't allow hitting in the classroom because we want everyone to be safe. Next time you can tell Tommy when you are angry." These explanations give words and direct links between actions and emotions. Children then begin to learn those connections and to use language to help understand and interpret the world around them (Howes and Ritchie 2002). For more in-depth explanation of therapeutic language you can use to build strong relationships, see the books *Unsmiling Faces: How Preschools Can Heal* by Lesley Koplow, or *A Matter of Trust: Connecting Teachers and Learners in the Early Childhood Curriculum* by

Using Your Words

Some of the most common ways to use words in a useful way with children who need consistency, emotional support, and security are described below.

1. Initial reactions: Instead of "Don't do that!" say, "Ouch! That hurts!" Instead of "That's not nice! No hitting!" say, "Remember, we don't hit here. If you are angry, use your words." (Koplow 2007)

2. Reflecting on emotions after the fact: "Do you remember when you were really mad at Julie when you were playing trucks?" (Koplow 2007)

3. Explanations of teacher decisions/behavior: "I'm going to stop you because . . ."; "I'm going to say no because . . ."; "I'm going to help you . . ." (Howes and Ritchie 2002)

4. Establishing boundaries: "I'm going to help you be safe . . ." (Koplow 2007)

5. Acknowledging emotions: "I know that makes you mad . . ."; "That must really hurt . . ." (Howes and Ritchie 2002)

6. Expressing consistency: "I know you're mad at me right now, but I'm still going to be here with you." (Koplow 2007)

Carollee Howes and Sharon Ritchie. Both books are great resources for more in-depth information that is outside the scope of this book.

During a sermon one Sunday, my pastor commented, "Sometimes we need help getting to the place where we can ask for help" (G. Berg-Moberg, personal communication, April 20, 2014). This struck me as especially relevant to caring for children experiencing trauma. One of the biggest challenges in working with these young children is that they do not have the words to articulate their experiences or feelings. Through giving them the words, building their understanding of the interplay of their emotions and behaviors, and coaching them on how to control those behaviors and emotions, you can provide the help that children need to get to the place where they can ask for help.

WHEN CAREGIVERS ARE PERPETRATORS AND VICTIMS OF VIOLENCE: DOMESTIC VIOLENCE

Mai came to my class refusing to speak to anyone. But her mother told me that Mai could speak in three different languages: Thai, Hmong, and English. I could tell early on that Mai was exceedingly bright. She followed instructions and easily mastered some of the more complicated matching and sorting games we played in the classroom. When I would tell a joke, she would scrunch up her face and giggle. She was clearly engaged in what was going on intellectually in the classroom, but she stuck pretty close to me and didn't make very many friends early in the year due in part to her refusal to speak to anyone in the classroom.

I eventually found out that Mai had witnessed the horrific torture of her mother at the hands of her father. In my mind, this was very likely the cause of Mai being selectively mute. From then on, I was able to focus my encouragement of Mai into building relationships with myself and other children to try to make sure she felt safe in the classroom. At a parent-teacher meeting with Mai and her mother, I expressed how much I wanted Mai to find a friend in the class. Mai seemed to take my words to heart, because soon afterward she began to play with some of the other children in the class. She slowly began to speak words and then short phrases, and joined in with the other children in the daily songs. I was thrilled that Mai felt safe enough to come out of her shell over the course of the year. By the end of the year, Mai passed the verbal naming test that she had failed early in the year. Her progress was remarkable, all because she felt safe and secure in the classroom environment we had built together.

—*A care provider's reflection*

Research

Mai is not alone in experiencing the challenges of witnessing domestic violence early in life. In the United States in 2006, an estimated 15.5 million children lived in homes where domestic violence had occurred during the past year (McDonald et al. 2006). Witnessing domestic violence not only puts children at increased risk for experiencing abuse themselves but also adds the complexity of observing a caregiver (usually the mother) being abused. For very young children who are dependent on their caregivers for survival, a threat to the mother may be perceived as a threat to the self. Children may have different reactions to being exposed to domestic violence. They may have difficulty reconciling the domestic violence and may think they are in some way responsible for the pain their family is experiencing. They may begin to blame themselves for the conflict in the home. They may feel overwhelmed by the conflict at home and seek to reestablish emotional security through relationships with others (Hungerford et al. 2012). In their attempts to connect with others, they may act aggressively or defensively, making social connections challenging.

As discussed in chapter 2, biological responses to threat include activation of the stress response system. A child may feel directly threatened by violence directed at a caregiver. Furthermore, the heightened stress response may be especially problematic for very young children who cannot yet regulate their emotions. Their dependence on a caregiver to help them deal with stress, coupled with a caregiver who is experiencing abuse, may result in a prolonged stress response, which can be detrimental to brain development (National Scientific Council on the Developing Child 2014).

More specifically, a number of poor outcomes have been associated with witnessing domestic violence in early life. Children exposed to domestic violence have been found to have lower IQ scores as well as academic difficulties. Toddlers exposed to domestic violence have shown poorer attention and memory skills than other toddlers. Furthermore, children who witness domestic violence may have difficulties with their peers and may have few friends (Hungerford et al. 2012). Children exposed to domestic violence may also be at risk for behavioral difficulties later in life, including internalizing (depression, anxiety) or externalizing (hyperactivity, aggression) behaviors. In addition, some research indicates that children who witness domestic violence are more likely to grow up thinking physical violence is acceptable. Young children learn through observing adults' behaviors. Thus, young children who witness domestic violence may learn that violence is an acceptable way to resolve conflict (Hungerford et al. 2012).

Children may be exposed to violence not only in their homes but also in their neighborhoods. Though less is known about the direct influence of neighborhood violence on children's development, it is clear that exposure to threats in the surrounding environment are detrimental to children. Unsafe neighborhoods can also mean fewer opportunities for enriching extracurricular activities. Gangs also pose a threat to children's safety because of the high exposure to guns, drugs, and other harmful experiences. Clearly, exposure to violence, or even just the consistent threat of violence, can have a huge impact on children's everyday lives (Lieberman et al. 2011).

Not surprisingly, evidence proves that children of mothers who are able to cope in the face of domestic violence and be responsive to their children's needs tend to show lower levels of subsequent behavior problems later in life. It seems that the mother's response and coping skills are imperative for supporting children's development in the context of domestic violence. The mother's ability to parent effectively and supportively in the context of domestic violence appears to be an important factor in a child's coping ability (Lieberman et al. 2011). This is especially true in early childhood, when children are predominantly dependent on their caregivers and have limited exposure to other adults in their everyday lives.

As a care provider, seeking ways to connect with and promote caregivers' relationships with their children can provide extra support for children who experience trauma. For example, in the case of Mai, the care provider spent a great deal of time building a relationship with Mai's mother and learned that Mai had witnessed her mother's torture at the hands of her father. Learning of this experience helped the care provider understand some of the reasons why Mai was extremely withdrawn in the classroom. In further working with Mai's mother, the care provider was able to build a more personalized plan to help Mai feel comfortable with making friends and talking in the classroom. Mai's mother, who was made aware of Mai's withdrawn tendencies in the classroom, could encourage Mai to participate more in the class. The relationship the care provider established with Mai's mother was crucial in successfully addressing Mai's needs and assuring Mai's mother of the safety of the care environment. Furthermore, it allowed for the coordination between the care provider and Mai's mother to foster Mai's development across the home and early care environments.

Response

Children who are exposed to neighborhood or domestic violence may exhibit very disturbing play themes. Guns and violence may enter the early care space through play despite attempts to curb these problematic themes. Dealing with these topics in the early care environment can be challenging. However, by maintaining structure and rules about violence in the care environment while acknowledging that violence is a very real part of some children's lives, you help to provide a safe space for all children to learn.

Consider Marcus, who is playing house with Gabby. Through your prior experience with Marcus, you suspect that he may be used to seeing women treated poorly. You watch carefully to make sure the play stays safe. Then you see Marcus reach out for Gabby and grab her arm, roughly pulling her toward him while yelling in her face. What do you do?

In a case like this, you may find it difficult not to let your own feelings and emotions get the better of you. Immediately and calmly intervening in this situation is challenging but necessary to ensure safety and also teach both children in the moment. To ensure the safety of Gabby, perhaps you separate the two children and check with Gabby to make sure she is okay. Then you might turn to Marcus and say, "Marcus, you can't grab Gabby and yell like that. That's too scary. We want to make sure everyone here feels safe." Keeping your tone firm but emotionally neutral is crucial. You might feel threatened or provoked, but by staying calm and engaged with Marcus, you can help him to regulate and understand his emotions and behaviors. Remember that each child is different, and strategies for working with one child may not work with another. However, through consistent engagement with children and experimenting with what works and what doesn't when they act out, you can tailor your responses to best meet the needs of each child (Gearity 2009).

Play is a potential healing place for children who have experienced trauma and loss. Play is a major developmental tool that children use to learn. It is where children can begin to explore complex relationships, feelings, scenarios, and social structures. Children's play often reflects their personal experience. Often in cases of traumatized children, play becomes very rigid and repetitive or has scary themes or events (Koplow 2007). Play themes may also be very dark in the case of trauma, especially in cases of exposure to violent acts. Reenacting traumatic events is common. Dealing with those play themes can be especially difficult when other children observe the play with wariness and apprehension. Establishing rules about what are appropriate play themes can be one way to curb these expressions of violence. Once children know what topics are off limits, you can more readily guide themes away from scary topics. Reminding and redirecting children to appropriate play themes can be useful: "Remember, José, we don't pretend to be killers here. That's too scary. Let's pretend to be animals instead." Children who are repetitively reenacting traumatic play may need extensive coaching and guidance on expanding their play to more developmentally appropriate topics.

Children who have experienced trauma may lack the necessary language for play. They may not be able to understand and interact with peers who are playing house because they have not learned the typical routines that are common in playing house. They may also lack the colorful variation that is often seen in young children's play. Children who have experienced trauma may limit themselves to games and tasks that have single purposes and don't require creativity of expression or interactions with peers. Other children who have experienced trauma may have violent outbursts of emotion or have difficulty remaining engaged in one activity for any length of time (Koplow 2007).

These behaviors may be off-putting for care providers and may be especially difficult to understand. Sometimes providers interpret children's lack of play to mean that they would be better off with very structured tasks instead of options for free play. Additionally, play may be seen as an unwelcome part of the care environment for children who have experienced trauma or loss, because of the potential for violent emotional outbursts or children hurting one another (Koplow 2007). However, the play environment gives providers opportunities for intervention with young children who have experienced trauma. Through constructing the play environment to convey safety, and to help children reorganize how they interpret and understand the scary events they have experienced, providers can help children begin to process the trauma.

Additionally, children who have disrupted play would benefit from working with a trained play therapist as a way to work through and process their experiences. Play therapy is a recognized technique used in a variety of contexts across early childhood (Koplow 2007). Becoming certified in play therapy is an important step in properly engaging in this therapeutic technique with young children. The discussion of the full therapeutic process of play therapy is outside the scope of this book. However, some techniques common in play therapy may be useful to providers. Play environments should have toys that are relational in nature (for example, dolls, play food, animals, telephones) and toys that may relate to children's actual experiences (for example, fire trucks, baby diapers, dress-up clothes, doctor's kit). Each of these items should have a specified "home" that the toys return to at the end of every play session. Maintaining a consistent rather than chaotic play environment is especially helpful for children who need structure and organization. Providers should be present when children are playing to provide input and redirection as needed, but also as a reminder of the presence of a consistent care provider (Koplow 2007). For children who have experienced trauma, having an adult present and available can be an important source of support.

In general, during play, the adult care provider can be a source of validation of emotions ("Oh, that must make baby scared!"), an active problem solver ("Oh, no! We're stuck and it's scary! What can we do?"), or an involved redirector of inappropriate behavior ("We don't play guns here. That's not safe. Let's take the guns and lock them up and build with the blocks instead.") (Howes and Ritchie 2002; Koplow 2007). Through providing explanation and validation of emotions, care providers help children understand that what they're feeling is acceptable. In being an active problem solver, the care provider engages with children to encourage them to come up with a solution to a problem. By establishing boundaries and redirecting play away from inappropriate themes, the care provider establishes norms of safety and appropriateness. These consistent interactions can help children who have experienced trauma to reorganize their understanding of the world and begin to practice how to play effectively. With the help of present and consistent providers, children can learn how to effectively communicate their feelings and needs, and appropriately engage in play with their peers (Koplow 2007).

WHEN FAMILIES ARE CHANGING: FOSTER CARE

In cases of extreme abuse, neglect, or domestic violence, children may be taken from their primary caregivers and placed in the foster care system. The goal of the foster care system is to place children into safe, temporary homes where they live until a permanent housing option can be secured, either through adoption or reunification with their primary caregivers.

Research

In 2012 a total of 399,546 children were in a foster care placement in the United States. This number was down almost 24 percent from the number of children in foster care in 2002 (US Department of Health and Human Services, Administration for Children and Families 2013). This decrease indicates that states are working to keep children with their biological families or seeking alternative placements (other members of the family) outside of traditional foster care homes. It is important to note, however, that racial and ethnic minorities are disproportionately represented in the foster care system. In 2012 almost 50 percent of the children placed in foster care identified as African American, Hispanic, American Indian, Hawaiian/Pacific Islander, or Asian (US Department of Health and Human Services, Administration for Children and Families 2013).

Though child welfare systems were created to protect and provide better care for children suffering the effects of maltreatment, these systems often become an added source of trauma and stress. Often systems become ineffective, or worse, detrimental, because of high caseloads, poorly trained or overstressed staff, or underresourced foster families (Masten 2014). When children are exposed to these environments, they experience added stress and adversity.

Because one of the most common reasons for placement in foster care is maltreatment, many children in foster care have histories of exposure to long-lasting, chronic traumatic experiences. This complex trauma means these children are in special need of stability and support to successfully overcome the negative effects of their traumatic experiences. Unfortunately, being placed in a foster care home does not ensure long-term stability.

Placement with one family long term is not always assured. In fact, many children transition through different foster placements regularly, and in some rare cases children end up in group homes or other institutionalized care settings. However, for very young children, placements in institutional settings are fairly rare, with approximately 90 percent of children between birth and age five placed in a family foster care setting (either with a relative or a nonrelative) (Anne E. Casey Foundation 2011).

Unfortunately, partly because of their emotional and behavioral issues, children experiencing complex trauma are even more likely to have repeated placements and disruptions to housing and family stability. Furthermore, when foster parents lack training and support from the child welfare system on how to handle children's emotional needs and disruptive behaviors, they may become overwhelmed and reject the child. This results in a series of potentially painful transitions from home to home, adding further stress and confusion to the trauma already experienced by these children. High rates of transition between home placements are not ideal for developing consistent, caring relationships, or for recovery from traumatic experiences (Spinazzola et al. 2013). Risks for poor health and behavior outcomes increase exponentially when children experience constant cycles of separation, potentially insufficient caregiving, and instability in placement. Furthermore, children can become traumatized in their new placement as a result of their experiences integrating with a new family (Spinazzola et al. 2013). The child welfare systems in many states are changing practices and policies to provide smoother transitions for children in foster care. Trauma-informed systems of care are also being implemented to better support children during emotional separation from their primary caregivers.

Children in foster care, by virtue of their experiences of trauma, are likely to face developmental challenges. Young children in foster care are at risk of experiencing toxic stress and subsequent changes to the developing brain. Children in foster care are significantly more likely to need treatment for psychological disorders such as depression and PTSD than their peers from families with low income who are not maltreated (Ai et al. 2013; Zeanah, Shauffer, and Dozier 2011). Furthermore, children who experience complex trauma are at higher risk for unemployment, early pregnancy, domestic violence, physical illness, and risky health behaviors later in life (Spinazzola et al. 2013). Because young children are so dependent on close, secure relationships with their caregivers for healthy development, it is very important that young children be placed in safe, stable, and responsive foster homes. Children who are suddenly separated from their primary caregiver may be fearful, withdrawn, and anxious, and may have difficulty sleeping (McAlister Groves 2013). These behaviors may be difficult for the foster parents to understand and deal with when they are attempting to build a relationship with the child.

Very young children are not able to maintain attachment relationships with biological parents with whom they are not in close, regular contact. The foster parent serves as a surrogate parent in a way that is different from foster parenting older children who can remember and maintain relationships with their biological parents across distance and time (Zeanah, Shauffer, and Dozier 2011). In some states, policy and practice changes include increased support and education for foster parents on the trauma that their foster children may experience and strategies for parenting highly stressed children. Without foster parents who provide safe and nurturing environments, children are at increased risk for developing insecure attachments, which may serve to exacerbate already existing traumatic stress responses in children.

Many young children may not understand why they are being taken away from their primary caregiver and may find the transition to foster care especially traumatic and challenging. Because very young children lack the ability to verbally express their emotions, they may have more difficulty understanding their experiences of separation and placement. Thus, special attention needs to be paid to helping young children process the transition (McAlister Groves 2013). In some cases, you as the child care provider may be one of the few consistent adult figures present throughout the child's transition process. You can thus play an important role in providing emotional stability and comfort to these children during times of great change.

Unfortunately, in some cases, foster care placements can be as threatening or abusive as the experiences the children were removed from. This is especially the case when multiple traumatized children are placed in the same care situation. Without adequate support, these children and adolescents may struggle to adopt healthy behaviors and may become perpetrators and victims of crimes in the foster home (Spinazzola et al. 2013).

Because positive relationships with supportive caregivers can be a transformative experience for children experiencing trauma, placing children into homes that meet their emotional needs can have significant positive effects on their later outcomes (Zeanah, Shauffer, and Dozier 2011). Stable, predictable environments for children who have experienced trauma are beneficial for supporting emotional and behavioral health (Spinazzola et al. 2013). Providing foster parents with adequate education, resources, and support throughout placement is essential to helping caregivers provide the best environment possible for traumatized children.

In many cases, reunification with the biological parents who are able to care for their children can also be beneficial to young children who have experienced trauma. Policies and practices in child welfare systems are shifting to encourage continued contact between biological parents and their children throughout foster care placement. When feasible, children should be enabled to maintain connections to their biological parents during placement to ensure as much stability in the transition between the foster and biological parent as possible (Wilson et al. 2011).

Response

Children who have experienced being in foster care have been through a number of disruptive transitions. Therefore, transitions between activities in the care environment may be a particularly relevant trigger for emotional and behavioral problems. In general, providing warning of an upcoming transition can be very beneficial (Howes and Ritchie 2002; Kaiser and Rasminsky 2012; Koplow 2007). Statements such as "In five minutes we're going to have story time," or "We'll have snacktime in three minutes. Let's clean up the cars. I will help you" can help cue the children to impending changes and make transitions more manageable. If transitions are unexpected—perhaps children were not aware of a change in the regular schedule—they can be especially problematic (Howes and Ritchie 2002). One way to help minimize distress is to maintain a clear and repetitive structure each day. When changes to the schedule occur, reminding children well ahead of time can help them deal with the stress of change ("Remember, tomorrow morning we're going to start with story time, not arts and crafts. I'll help you remember tomorrow too"). In addition, it may be useful for some children who have difficulty with transitions to carry a special toy, stuffed animal, or blanket as a "transitional object." These transitional objects can provide comfort to children during the stress of the transition. With these objects they may be more likely to be able to self-soothe and effectively decrease their arousal (Howes and Ritchie 2002). In addition, if you are able to stay with the child during a transition, this can provide an added level of security and safety.

Being very explicit about the steps necessary for the child to make a transition from one activity to another can be very beneficial. Some children may have trouble keeping a sequence of behaviors in mind long enough to successfully complete them. For example, Linea may struggle with cleaning up from playtime, getting her coat from her cubby, and lining up to go outside for recess. Providing Linea with prompts about upcoming transitions is helpful: "Linea, in five minutes you need to line up for recess." In addition, reminding her of all the steps she needs to take to line up can be useful: "Linea, remember, first you need to put the toys away. I'll help you." Then, once the toys are put away, you might say, "Okay, you need to go to your cubby and get your coat and line up for recess." This type of instruction helps Linea keep multiple steps in mind and not get distracted in the process. She may require even more direct instruction, such as "Linea, you need to go get your coat from your cubby. Then come back here to me, please." Once Linea returns to you with her coat, you could finish the instruction with "Okay, now you can go line up for recess." Sometimes providing these multiple steps seems tedious; however, they may also prevent meltdowns and frustrations for both you and the child.

Children in foster care likely have also gone through other traumatic experiences (for example, maltreatment, death of parents or guardians). Therefore, considering not only the effect of the foster placement but also the potential impact of children's other traumatic experiences on their behaviors is vital. Children's lives have been significantly disrupted in the case of foster care, and likely they have been removed from their primary attachment figures. Thus, children may be experiencing difficulties understanding and forming new relationships with adults. If you suspect this is the case, focusing on relationship building with the child will be necessary. Many of the relationship-building strategies are consistent with the suggestions throughout this book. Ensuring safety, structure, rules, and acknowledgment of feelings can go a long way in communicating to children that you care for them. However, in the case of children experiencing foster care, verbally saying that you care about them may be especially helpful. Saying things like "I care about you, so I'm going to stay here with you" can communicate not only that you care but also that you will be present with them when they need you (Howes and Ritchie 2002).

Despite your best efforts, you will not be able to curb all emotional meltdowns and behavioral outbursts. Some responses to children during these behavioral challenges may be more effective at diffusing emotionally charged situations than others. For example, one fairly standard approach to addressing a behavioral outburst might be to send the child away from the group for a time-out. Typically this approach is used to interrupt undesirable behavior and provide an opportunity for the child to take a break from the activity causing the undesirable behavior (Gearity 2009). This may involve the child sitting in a corner alone, apart from the group, so he can "think about his actions." However, this method of discipline may make children who already have safety and security concerns feel ashamed, or that their feelings and needs are not important to the provider. Children who have experienced trauma may perceive this time-out as further evidence of adult hostility toward them. For children who have been neglected or who have unstable relationships with adults in their lives, this type of isolation may be especially upsetting and counterproductive (Gearity 2009; Koplow 2007). A traditional time-out of this type could potentially lead to even further challenges with the teacher-child relationship. Additionally, this separation method effectively disengages children from the learning environment and their peers. Instead, working directly with children to provide help in resolving conflict with a peer or in a challenging activity may decrease frustration and emotionality in children and help them reengage in learning and play. However, this must always be done within the structure of the rules of the classroom (Jacobson 2008). Classroom rules, especially those regarding safety, need to be upheld to maintain structure and stability in the classroom.

For example, imagine that Demetrius and Latoya are playing in the block area. Demetrius becomes upset and hurls a block at Latoya while yelling a curse word. The care provider immediately separates the children to prevent any further injury. She checks quickly to see if Latoya is hurt and then addresses Demetrius: "Demetrius, I see that you're mad. But we don't throw things, because it's not safe. We need to keep everyone safe. I'm going to stay with you over here until you can calm down and play safely." Demetrius, still upset, follows the teacher to another, quieter area of the classroom where she proceeds to talk with him quietly until he is calmer and can return to playing with the blocks.

In this scenario, Demetrius's actions may have stemmed from his being too aroused by the loud, stimulating play environment. Because he couldn't control his behaviors, he lashed out at Latoya, throwing a block at her and yelling. Instead of viewing this as a belligerent, intentional act, the teacher understood that Demetrius may have been overstimulated and that he does not have the skills to regulate his own emotions when stressed.

Had the teacher demanded that Demetrius go to time-out alone in the corner to think about his actions, he may have continued to feel out of control. He might also have felt that his care provider was being hostile toward him. In cases like these, if children must be separated because they are a danger to themselves or others, it is a good idea to have a care provider stay with them until they are able to calm down (Howes and Ritchie 2002). Then children are not socially isolated, but rather begin to learn how to cope with their emotions through the presence and coaching from a caring adult.

Often, discerning how best to engage with a child who is expressing challenging behaviors can be difficult in the moment. However, one way to work through especially challenging encounters with young children is to use four questions to guide your response.

1. What is the child doing? (assessing)
   In the case of Demetrius, he was being unsafe by throwing a block and yelling profanity. Because he was being unsafe, he needed to be corrected immediately.
2. What are you feeling? (self-monitoring)
   If you're Demetrius's teacher and this is not the first time this type of thing has happened, you may feel a sense of frustration. You may be fearful that Latoya has been injured. You may feel angry that despite your previous efforts, Demetrius continues to act out.

3. What is the relevant context? (previous observation)

You know that Demetrius, though he is four, acts more like a two- or three-year-old, especially during free-play time when there is a lot of noise and activity in the classroom. He seems to have trouble controlling his behavior, especially during this time of day. You know he has been exposed to his parents' criminal activity and some neighborhood violence, and you suspect that his parents do not pay much attention to him at home.

4. What are your options? (acting)

You know you must immediately separate Demetrius from Latoya and uphold the rules of safety in the classroom. Knowing that he struggles to control his own emotions, you suspect that your presence and coaching may be necessary for him to get himself back under control. You decide to separate him from other children but to stay with him until he has calmed down (Howes and Ritchie 2002; Koplow 2007).

CONCLUSIONS

Maltreatment and domestic violence are prominent types of trauma that very young children may experience that can have long-lasting effects on the brain and behavior. These complex traumas are especially problematic because they disrupt important caregiver-child attachment relationships. For children who have experienced maltreatment, foster care placements may provide an opportunity for promoting positive change or be perpetuators of adversity. However, where children who have experienced trauma are able to develop safe, supportive relationships with caregivers, either biological or in foster care, they are more likely to thrive later on.

A variety of types of treatments are available for children who have experienced trauma that may significantly increase their likelihood of successfully overcoming its effects. Discussion of these treatments is outside the scope of this book. However, resources can be found on my website (www.drlangworthy.com) that provide more comprehensive information on how to work with children who have experienced various forms of trauma.

LINGERING QUESTIONS

➤ **I am working with a child who I suspect is being abused or neglected. What do I do?** If you believe the child is a victim of abuse, you should report it to the proper authorities in your state (see https://www .childwelfare.gov/responding/reporting.cfm for information on how to report a case of suspected maltreatment). If you believe the case involves domestic violence against one of the parents and you feel comfortable reaching out to the parent, you can encourage the parent to seek services or to call the National Domestic Violence Hotline at 1-800-799-7233 for help.

➤ **When I hear the horrifying things that children in my care have experienced, I feel very upset and don't know how to respond. What do I do?** First, it is completely understandable and acceptable for you to feel upset hearing about these experiences. In the immediate moment, taking a deep, calming breath can help steady you and bring your heart rate back to normal. When you talk with children, focus on emphasizing their safety in your care environment, and acknowledge any feelings of fear or anger they may have. Avoid making promises you can't keep (such as "It's all going to be okay").

➤ **Do all traumatic experiences cause toxic stress?** No. Though in many cases we can assume that a person experiences increased levels of stress when exposed to maltreatment and violence, the degree of damage that stress has on the brain and body depends largely on children's surrounding relationships. If children are surrounded by caring, responsive adults who can buffer them from the effects of the stressful situations, they experience tolerable stress and can recover from traumatic events. However, if children do not have those supportive, caring environments, they may experience more toxic levels of stress.

6 When Those Who Love Us Leave Us

I'm glad we had the times together just to laugh and sing a song, seems like we just got started and then before you know it, the times we had together were gone.

DR. SEUSS

 June runs toward me, boisterous and smiling. She's wearing her pajamas again, I notice, with no socks, her slippered feet sliding across the floor as she scampers to the art corner. Though her mother died two years ago, probably before June could even remember her, I suspect her mother's suicide will have a lasting effect on her. Once the other children are settled, I walk over to the art area to see that she's picked up a blue crayon and has begun drawing.

"That's a very nice picture, June," I say, bending down next to her.

"My mama likes blue. I'm going to show it to her when I get home," she replies. She sticks her tongue out slightly, deep in concentration on the work of art in front of her.

This isn't the first time she's spoken of her mother this way. I still remember the shock I felt when I first heard her speak about her mother as if her mother were alive. That first time, I was quick to remind her that her mother had died. The second those words left my mouth, I wished I could have taken them back.

Now, as I look at June's picture of what appears to be a group of bright blue flowers, I crouch down beside her, saying softly, "Remember, June, your mama is in heaven now." I pause as she continues to scribble. "You really love your mama, don't you?"

"Yeah, she's going to love my picture. She's going to come down from heaven to see me."

I pause a moment, gauging the best response. I finally settle on "It would be so nice if she could come down from heaven and be with you. That would make you so happy."

June nods excitedly and continues drawing.

I leave her to her coloring, making my rounds to check in on the other children, pondering June's response to my reminder of her mother's absence. She's brought this up repeatedly. It has occasionally become a distraction to her own as well as other children's learning. In my thirty years of teaching, I've never had a student who referred to a deceased parent as being alive. I don't really know how to deal with this issue, but I strive to affirm June's feelings all the while gently reminding her of the fact that her mother is gone.

Caught in my own thoughts, I don't hear June approach. She tugs my sleeve, and when I turn to her, she stretches her arm up to me, holding her drawing proudly, beaming.

I smile down at her. "That's beautiful, June! Why don't you put it in your cubby so you can bring it home for your daddy to see."

June nods excitedly and dashes off to her cubby, her slippered feet sliding swiftly across the floor.

I call all the children together. It's story time. I know today I'll let the children choose a book about trains, or plants, or maybe zoo animals. The book about families can wait for another day.

—*Scene based on reflections of a care provider*

LOSS

June's story is not uncommon. Perhaps you have felt the piercing pain of grief at seeing a young child ripped from a parent too soon. Many children experience prolonged or permanent separation from their primary caregivers early in life. As with maltreatment, the loss of a primary caregiver can be traumatic for young children. As a care provider, what do you do? How do you respond when a child is confused about a parent's death or absence?

There are no easy answers when children are dealing with the trauma of loss. Loss can take many forms: loss of home and shelter, separation from parents due to parental incarceration or military deployment, or the death of a caregiver. These are all major experiences of loss that many children endure. For very young children, this can be especially troubling, as they are just beginning to learn about the world around them. As established in chapter 1, serve-and-return relationships are crucial factors in the early development of cognitive, social, and emotional skills. Young children may not have the language to express their feelings of sadness and grief. Instead, their distress is often conveyed through challenging behaviors. This chapter will unpack some of those difficult behaviors and explore research evidence on the effects of the trauma of different kinds of loss young children experience.

WHEN THE ONES WE LOVE DIE: COPING WITH THE DEATH OF A PARENT

The death of a parent unceremoniously rips young children away from a primary source of care, comfort, and security. The loss of a parent is a huge blow to young children, and the finality of the loss is often difficult to communicate to them (Lieberman and Van Horn 2013). Children may also question

their own responsibility for the death of their parent, wondering if they were somehow the cause. We have limited understanding of how young children process death, but in general children seem to go through stages of protest, despair, and detachment similar to an extended separation from a parent (Lieberman and Van Horn 2013). Practitioners have developed resources and methods of working with children who have experienced a parent's death (Miller, Rosengren, and Gutierrez 2014). As a result, we have a greater understanding of how adults can help children process their grief and begin to move forward from the significant loss.

Research

The death of a parent may be one of the most stressful experiences young children can endure. Not only do children lose a primary attachment figure who cared for their physical needs, but they also lose someone with whom they were emotionally linked. Additionally, as a result of the parent's death, children may experience difficulties in other areas of their lives. With the loss may come increasing economic hardship, moving to a new place, and changing child care environments. This loss of stability is an additional disruption to children's lives (Miller, Rosengren, and Gutierrez 2014).

Children who have experienced a parent's death will likely experience shock and denial immediately following the loss. This may soon shift to anger and sadness, which may last for several months. After a period of grieving, children will usually find some kind of acceptance and readjust to their new lives without the parent. The length of the grieving period for losing a parent varies from child to child (Miller, Rosengren, and Gutierrez 2014). If children are encountering other traumatic experiences in addition to the loss of a parent, they may exhibit more severe behavioral and emotional challenges as well as depression and anxiety. Some research has indicated an increased rate of suicidal thoughts and tendencies in older children who have lost a parent. However, researchers conclude that these suicidal thoughts are generally more out of a desire to be reunited with their parent than out of feelings of worthlessness or hopelessness (Dowdney 2000). Many children may also experience sleeplessness, guilt, and social and behavioral challenges. Little research evidence exists to suggest increased anxiety disorders in children who have experienced a parent's death, though children may express worries about the possibility of the death of their other parent (Dowdney 2000).

Talking with children about the death can be extremely uncomfortable and emotionally difficult for adults. The remaining parents experience their own grief, in addition to dealing with the grief of their children. This places considerable burden on the parents. There is also a wish to protect their children from further pain. Young children may forget or have a hard time grasping the concept that their parents will never return. Having to constantly remind children that their parents will not be returning may feel harsh to adults. However, clinicians and researchers have found that talking honestly with children about the loss is beneficial for their grieving (Dowdney 2000; Lieberman and Van Horn 2013; Miller, Rosengren, and Gutierrez 2014). Having these difficult conversations can be taxing for everyone involved but eventually will help children grasp the reality of the loss and begin to work through their thoughts and emotions.

Many contextual factors can affect how children process the loss of a parent. The closeness of the relationship to the parent is a factor that may contribute to how children grieve. For example, if a child does not know the parent because of divorce, separation or estrangement, the child may not seem to be affected much by the death of the parent. Conversely, if a child has a close bond with the parent, or if the parent is the main attachment figure, the loss will likely be felt very strongly.

How a parent died may also affect a child's grief. Whether the loss is from a prolonged illness or a sudden accident may influence how a child processes and grieves the loss. In the case of a prolonged illness, parents and children may have a chance to discuss and prepare (to whatever extent possible) for the impending loss (Dowdney 2000). Whether the parent was murdered, committed suicide, or died in an accident may affect the way the child understands the parent's death. Children may question how they might have prevented the accident or murder, or why their parents would want to take their own lives. If the child witnessed the parent's murder or suicide, the child's risk for later psychological problems such as PTSD may depend on the child's traumatic response to that experience (Dowdney 2000; Lieberman and Van Horn 2011). If a parent is killed during military service, the already prolonged separation may increase the child's struggle with the idea that the parent is never coming back (Lieberman and Van Horn 2013).

Children of different ages will process the loss differently. Very young children will likely have more difficulty understanding the finality and permanency of death than older children and adolescents. Young children are also more likely to exhibit regressive behaviors (bed-wetting, age-inappropriate behaviors) and have explosive emotions, temper tantrums, overall irritability and impatience, extreme shyness, or disinterest in play (Dowdney 2000; Miller, Rosengren, and Gutierrez 2014). Older youth may exhibit more classic signs of clinical depression. Boys may also show increased aggressive and acting-out behaviors, whereas girls are more likely to show sadness or decreased engagement in activities (Dowdney 2000). In addition, if children already have a psychological illness, the loss of parent is likely to aggravate those difficulties and increase the chances for more severe illness later.

How the surviving parent copes with the loss is also a factor in the child's response to the trauma. The surviving parent or other adults who care for the child may face their own psychological grief of the loss. As a result, they may find it difficult to meet the increased needs of the child. Children may begin to feel even more detached from their primary caregivers, and subsequently not receive the necessary support and security they require from these relationships. Furthermore, the loss may put children in the role of not only dealing with their own grief, but also caring for the surviving parent's emotional health if the parent experiences depression, anxiety, or PTSD as a result of the loss (Dowdney 2000). Thus, it is very important for surviving caregivers to have access to family, friends, and other social supports to process their own grief so they may then provide the best support they can for their children. The more caregivers are supported, the more they are able to build their children's resilience to loss through providing responsive, sensitive care.

Cultural beliefs about death are also a major factor in how children process and understand the loss of a parent. Some cultures are very open about death with young children, and children are an integral part of the mourning process. Other cultures tend to try to protect children from death, believing they are better off not participating in the mourning practices. Though some clinicians recommend that children participate in mourning the loss of their loved one (attending the parent's funeral), cultural beliefs and ethnic traditions should be considered before recommending any specific course of action in dealing with children's grief (Dowdney 2000).

Response

Children who experience the loss of a loved one will go through periods of intense grief and sadness. In general, this is expected. However, it is important to identify any atypical behavior and also provide support to children as they go through the grieving process. In general, with young children you can expect the following types of behaviors:

- preoccupation with how the loved one died
- reenacting the death in play or artwork
- emotional distress when reminded of the death
- avoidance of reminders (people, places, activities, locations) of the loss
- withdrawing and disengaging from activities
- numbness or "flat" emotions
- being easily startled or jumpy
- loss of purpose and meaning in life (NCTSN 2004)

Children who are struggling with the loss of a parent may have a lot of questions. Listening calmly to those questions and providing comforting and truthful, direct responses may help children to process their emotions. You may be tempted to avoid the words "death" or "died" when talking about loss with children. However, these words are often more helpful to children than saying more ambiguous phrases like "He went away" or "She went to sleep for a long time." These statements are likely to be confusing to children processing loss (NCTSN 2004). In addition, you should provide emotion-affirming statements, such as "You miss your mommy very much" or "I know you are sad." This language can help children better understand and process their feelings of grief. The more you can remain emotionally open and available, the more you can help grieving children feel safe and secure.

Children who have experienced loss are also likely to have outbursts and express anger. This is normal while children work through their grief. Calmly addressing these outbursts in a nonpunitive manner. Nevertheless, rules and structures should still be maintained. Similarly, children may need additional help entering or staying engaged in activities. When children experience numbness and withdraw from activities, provide a way to reengage with the activities in a sensitive manner. In other words, you might say things like "Tony, can you help me put the stickers on the paper? I need your help to make it pretty," or "Li, let's go play house with Kayla. We can go together."

You will find value in being in contact with the family about cultural and family traditions throughout the grieving period. For some people, grief and loss are very private experiences that are not typically discussed in social situations. For others, sympathies from people around them may be a welcome comfort. Letting other children in the care environment know that the child has experienced a loss may be useful. You might explain to the other children why the grieving child may have many different feelings. However, ensure that your explanations are within the parameters of the family's wishes. Maintaining contact with the family is key in understanding the family's needs for how best to support the child through these difficult times (NCTSN 2004).

WHEN BATTLES MUST BE FOUGHT: PARENTAL MILITARY DEPLOYMENT

Unfortunately, war is a constant part of human existence. Military troops are sent across the world to resolve conflicts and protect national interests. Many of these troops serving in the military have families and children whom they leave behind for months at a time during deployments. Some estimates indicate that 41 percent of active duty service members and about 25 percent of reserve service members have children who are between birth and five years of age (Lieberman and Van Horn 2013). Often these troops are risking their lives, and some never return home to their loved ones. Considerable research has documented the psychological and emotional toll that military service can place on veterans. Many veterans struggle with mental health concerns after returning from combat, and those who were physically injured face the challenges associated with physical disability. Military veterans may also struggle with reintegration into normal life postcombat and may face substance abuse problems. Though increased attention has been paid to the challenges military service personnel face since the recent conflicts in Iraq and Afghanistan, less is known about the impact on the children and families who support these troops (Gewirtz et al. 2011).

Research

Families supporting their deployed military family members face an array of challenges and stressors. These challenges may change at different points in the deployment process. Before a family member leaves for service, the family must prepare for the lengthy absence of one of the primary caregivers. A great deal of stress and uncertainty may surround the length and location of deployment. Additionally, changes to child care may be necessary as a single parent is left to care for the family during the other parent's deployment. The preparation for deployment may also cause parents to be highly focused on preparing for separation and less focused on their children's need to understand what is happening (Lieberman and Van Horn 2013). As discussed in chapter 1, young children rely on caregivers' responsiveness and emotional states to evaluate their own safety and security. If parents are stressed and emotional, young children may feel distressed and act out those feelings. Children's challenging behaviors may increase parental frustration, further straining the parents' relationships with their children. Talking with children about the impending separation and discussing the children's feelings about the parent leaving may be a helpful strategy for parents (Lieberman and Van Horn 2013).

The first month of separation may be the most challenging time for some families. Feelings of loss, anxiety, and sleeplessness are common. For young children, this time may be especially challenging, as they may not fully understand the separation from the deployed parent, and they may be worried that their other parent may also leave them. Some research indicates that in this first month after deployment, children exhibit more extreme behavioral outbursts. After the first month, some of these challenges seem to fade as a new version of normal life is achieved. However, some children have persistent behavioral problems throughout the deployment (Gewirtz et al. 2011; Lieberman and Van Horn 2013).

Throughout the deployment process, families of the service member may experience chronic stress. They may experience worry about the safety of the deployed family member, economic hardships, and the strain of single parenting (Gewirtz et al. 2011). The increasing behavioral and emotional demands from children may place additional stress on the parent at home who is already strained under the emotional toll of separation. Given the compounding levels of stress in the home, it is not surprising that child maltreatment rates increase during deployment (Gewirtz et al. 2011; Lieberman and Van Horn 2013). Accessing social support from others is an important process for parents who are struggling.

Reunification after a parent returns from deployment, though joyful for the whole family, can also be challenging. As service members begin the process of reintegrating into their homes and families, a period of "relearning" occurs. Parents must reacquaint themselves with each other and must work out new roles as caregivers. Children must also get to know their parent again and learn that the parent may not be exactly as they remembered. Likewise, the returning parent must learn about all of the changes in the child's life. Often this period is very challenging for parents and children. Child maltreatment rates also increase during the reintegration period (Lieberman and Van Horn 2013). Throughout this time, parents need to be patient with one another as well as with their children to work through the emotional transition that occurs during reintegration.

Reintegration can be further complicated by parental injury or mental illness. Young children may need to learn that their parent has limited physical ability and may express concern or anxiety about the physical injury. Furthermore, in many cases, the injured parent must go through prolonged hospitalization and rehabilitation. This may occur away from the family, thus increasing the length of separation (Lieberman and Van Horn 2013). In the case of mental illness or substance abuse, there is likely to be considerable strife between parents, adding further stress to the reintegration process. Children may struggle with understanding why their parent is sad and distant, or why the parent may react unpredictably in certain situations. In these

cases, it is extremely important for families to have support from friends, family, and service providers to enable the smoothest transition.

As with most children who experience the loss or disruption of a primary attachment relationship, children of military parents may struggle with the sense of loss as well as with the uncertainty of their parent's return. This may result in increased uncertainty about their own security. Additionally, children may understand the potential threat to their parent's life during deployment. As discussed in chapter 5, for very young children, a threat to the caregiver is often interpreted as a threat to the self. Children in military families may experience increased anxiety, feelings of helplessness, depression, or PTSD due to the separation and uncertainty that accompanies a parent's deployment (Paris et al. 2010).

One of the primary factors that successfully predicts a family's success in navigating stressful situations like military deployment is the caregivers' ability to effectively respond to children's emotional needs. Substantial research has documented that responsive parenting provides a buffer for children in times of great stress (National Research Council and Institute of Medicine 2000). A variety of interventions and social supports are available to military families (see my website, www.drlangworthy.com, for more information) that can help provide parents with strategies to deal with the stress they experience before, during, and after deployment.

Response

As a child care provider, you may encounter children who have parents deployed in the military. You may notice swings in behavior and mood based on where the family is in the deployment cycle. The strategies listed below are some things that you can do as a care provider to help support children throughout the deployment process.

- Maintain rules and routines. Added structure and consistency will increase stability for the child.
- Respond to the child's anxiety. Children's fears about their parents' well-being are very real. Responding in a caring, supportive manner, while also reassuring children that the military is doing everything they can to keep the parent safe, can provide comfort to children.
- Minimize transitions. Children in military families may experience frequent moves and transitions, especially leading up to a deployment. Parents may seek to move children from one care situation

to another that is closer or more convenient. However, such transitions can be very stressful for young children. Providing as much flexibility as possible for these families to reduce these transitions is beneficial.

- Be aware of possible reminders and triggers. Topics of free play (for example, playing war) or talk about guns or tanks may be a reminder of the danger to the parent during deployment. Trying to maintain a safe environment free of traumatic reminders is beneficial for these children.

- Keep children engaged in activities. This may mean sitting with them to keep them focused or providing extra encouragement and praise when children remain engaged. You can also sensitively bring children back into the activity or conversation when they disengage (Gewirtz et al. 2011; Lieberman and Van Horn 2013; Paris et al. 2010; NCTSN, n.d.-b).

Children may be worried about the safety of the parent who is deployed and ask questions like "Will my daddy die?" It is important to avoid statements and promises that you cannot guarantee, like "I'm sure he'll be okay" or "He'll come home safe." These types of statements may feel reassuring in the moment, but if the parent does not return safely, this can be detrimental to the child's coping. Stick with statements like "I know you're scared for your daddy. People are doing everything they can to keep him safe," or "You miss your mommy a lot. She misses you too. She wants to come home safe." Additionally, assuring children of their own safety in your care environment can help allay their fears about their own security (Lieberman and Van Horn 2013). In addition to providing support to the child, it can be helpful to talk with the parent to get some information about the deployment. Furthermore, you can encourage the family to maintain rules and routines at home, provide insights into the child's feelings and coping, and offer assistance in minimizing transitions (Gewirtz et al. 2011). Developing collective strategies to best support children and families will help them cope with the process of deployment.

PARENTS IN PRISON: INCARCERATION

 "My mom's in jail! My mom's in jail! My mom's in jail!" Tyrell's voice rings out across the classroom as he hops up and down from one foot to the other, knocking over blocks and stepping on stuffed animals. The other children playing around him look up at him, baffled. Some of them have never heard of jail. Others have heard only that it's a place where bad people go.

"Tyrell, I need you to stop jumping. It's time to sit and play with the blocks." His teacher, Ms. Mary, calls out from across the room, moving to intercept him just as he trips on a block and tumbles to the floor. He's up again before she can reach him, this time dashing across the room as if to hide from her.

"No!" he screams, as if suddenly terrified. "No! Don't take me there! I don't wanna go!"

"Tyrell, you can come over here and sit with me for a little while," the teacher says, finally reaching where Tyrell has hidden himself in the corner of the room. But by this point, Tyrell is inconsolable, crying loudly, saying, "No, no, no, no!" The teacher speaks softly to him, and he seems to calm down momentarily.

I hear him say, "My mom is gonna come get me today. She's gonna take me and my sister for ice cream."

The teacher corrects him, reminding him that his mother is far away but that she still loves him very much.

"No! I'm gonna see her! I want to see her now!" Tyrell bursts into another fit of tears. The teacher settles next to him, holding him close.

I wish I could say this was uncommon. But Tyrell's behavior is consistently inconsistent. He persistently asks questions about his mom, or seems to forget that she's in jail but then the next moment loudly discloses to the entire room full of people where his mom is. He feels the immense loss of her but doesn't understand why she's gone. I know it's all been very confusing and unsettling for him.

Tyrell sees me now, his blotchy tearful eyes finding mine across the room. He leaps up from Ms. Mary's lap and sprints over to greet me, a big grin on his face. He knows me. As his guardian ad litem, I'm one of the few consistent faces he's seen over the last few months. I quickly scoop him up, giving him a tight hug as he clings to me for dear life.

Ms. Mary approaches, saying, "Thank you for coming. I appreciate you being willing to meet with me about Tyrell."

"Of course," I reply, smiling. "Anything for Tyrell."

I know how this goes; I've been in these meetings before. She'll say, "His behavior is disruptive and unpredictable. His outbursts about his mother's situation disturb the other children. I'm not sure what to say to him about his mother."

"He deserves better than the hand he's been dealt," I think to myself as I look down at the boy now happily playing with the buttons on my cardigan. He got caught in the cross fire of someone else's mistake. And I know we can do better for him.

I take a deep breath and hope that Ms. Mary will believe that too.

—*Scene based on reflections of a guardian ad litem*

Children who have parents who are incarcerated (in prison or jail) are largely an invisible population. In the past, researchers, practitioners, and professionals have focused very little on how incarceration of a parent might impact young children. However, estimates from 2007 indicate that approximately one in forty-three children in the United States has a parent who is currently incarcerated (Maruschak, Glaze, and Mumola 2010). Essentially, that's one child in every other classroom. That rate is higher than the rates of both juvenile diabetes and autism in the United States. There are also disproportionately more minorities than whites in the prison system. A staggering one in fifteen African American children has a parent who is incarcerated (Maruschak, Glaze, and Mumola 2010). Yet parental incarceration receives very little attention in the public sphere.

Research

Children with incarcerated parents present many of the same cognitive, social, emotional, and behavioral difficulties as other children who have experienced the loss of a caregiver. Children of incarcerated parents are at increased risk for depression, anxiety, and delinquency behaviors (Shlafer et al. 2013). They may also experience cognitive delays and social difficulties. Children of incarcerated parents may come from economically disadvantaged situations or experience abuse or neglect. In addition, their parents may struggle with substance abuse, mental or physical illness, or their own experiences of maltreatment. Some research indicates that having a parent who is incarcerated increases the risk for later antisocial behaviors on the part of the child (Shlafer et al. 2013). Furthermore, having an incarcerated parent was one of the adverse early experiences categories in the Adverse Childhood Experiences (ACE) study. Having an incarcerated parent, in conjunction with other risk factors, was linked to physical and mental health difficulties later in life (Felitti et al. 1998).

Some children of incarcerated parents may have witnessed the arrest of their parent. This can be an extremely stressful and traumatic experience for children, as they may have witnessed police showing up with weapons drawn. In other cases, children or other members of their families may have been the victims of the criminal activity. This further complicates the children's experiences because of the perceived threat on primary caregivers and family members. In one study, more than one-third of inmates reported that their children had been present during their criminal activity, arrest, or sentencing (Shlafer et al. 2013; Dallaire and Wilson 2010). These experiences may be especially difficult for very young children, as they may not understand the emotionally charged situation or why their parent is being taken away from them.

Children may also struggle because of the stigma associated with incarceration. They may be uncomfortable talking about their parent but may also experience feelings of sadness or anger at the loss of their parent. In the early care environment, it is common to have children share with one another about their families. For example, when asked to share about what his father does for a living, Jamal, whose father is incarcerated, becomes very ashamed. He sheepishly admits his daddy is in jail because his daddy did a bad thing. The teacher may also become uncomfortable, not only because of Jamal's admission, but also because it may spur other children to ask questions about what jail is and why Jamal's dad is there.

Conversely, some parents may not tell their children the truth about where their parent is during the incarceration. Some parents may say things like "He went away to college" or "She's on a long trip for work." This can be especially challenging if the child finds out from another person that the parent is incarcerated. This lie may breed feelings of anger and mistrust and cause added confusion and frustration. Many professionals recommend that parents be open and honest with their children about the parent's incarceration, as it helps the child process what incarceration means for the family (Shlafer et al. 2013).

The effects of having an incarcerated parent are dependent on a variety of factors, including age. For example, for an infant or toddler, having a mother who is incarcerated may present unique challenges because the mother is likely to be the child's primary attachment figure. This primary reliance may make a separation from the mother especially problematic. Infants and young children also have limited ability to understand the reasons for the parent's departure and have fewer emotional skills to process the experience. Older children have a greater capacity to understand and process the incarceration of the parent (Shlafer et al. 2013).

Furthermore, when a child's primary caregiver is incarcerated, many transitions must occur. There may be shifts in housing, changes in school or child care arrangements, transitions to another household, entrance into the foster care system, or increased economic hardship. The disruptive nature of these transitions can have detrimental effects on young children who are already experiencing loss (Shlafer et al. 2013). However, some of those effects can be lessened by the presence of stable, caring family members or other adults who help to support the family and children through these difficult transitions. The importance of maintaining as much stability as possible during a parent's incarceration, especially for very young children, cannot be overstated.

The degree to which a relationship can be maintained with the parent who is incarcerated may have an important role in how the child responds to the incarceration. Unfortunately, visits with the parent may be complicated by the distance to where the parent is being held, the visitation policies of the jail or prison, the rules about mail or phone calls, and the unwelcoming nature of some visitation areas (Shlafer et al. 2013). As highlighted previously, some parents do not even reveal the incarcerated parent's status to their children. In those cases, children are not able to visit their parent at all during the incarceration. Some families may maintain contact with one another via phone or mail. Other children may not be able to visit their parent because of the distance to the facility or the cost or logistics of traveling there. Those who are able to visit may experience the frustrations of complicated rules during visitation (no baggy sweatshirts, no touching, no toys). Rules vary by each prison or jail system. In some cases, the parent and child may briefly hug and kiss, and then must sit opposite from one another for the remainder of the visit. In other facilities, the incarcerated parent is separated from visitors by a plexiglass window. Though maintaining security is crucial, children may not understand why they can't hug and touch their parent, and may become frustrated and cause a disturbance, which can lead to revoking visitation privileges. Though some visitation rooms do have toys and family activities, many do not. Some visitation areas are very stark and unfriendly places, potentially frightening for young children. Indeed, visitation can be a stressful experience for children (Shlafer et al. 2013).

Response

Children's experience of a parent's incarceration may vary significantly based on a variety of factors. Some children may be able to visit their parents while they are incarcerated, whereas others may only get the occasional phone call. It can be useful to find out the details of the incarcerated parent's relationship with the child; whether the child was present during the criminal activity, arrest, or sentencing of the parent; and whether the child has experienced instability during the incarceration. These are important factors in understanding the individual child's situation and how you as a care provider can best work with that child (Shlafer et al. 2013).

In the case of Tyrell described earlier in this section, he was clearly having difficulty understanding and dealing with his mother being in jail. He went from proclaiming in a singsong voice to the entire room of children that his mom was in jail to insisting that he would see his mother later that night at home. This apparent dissociation might be startling to some teachers. As in the case of military deployment or the death of a parent, children may have difficulty grasping the reality of a parent being away for an extended period of time. Furthermore, as some parents try to withhold this information or do not wish their children to be aware of the circumstances of the incarceration, your job as a provider becomes even more complicated. Children may act out frightening scenarios of the criminal activity or the arresting event, potentially scaring other children. As discussed in chapter 5, it is important that you maintain boundaries on acceptable types of play, while also helping the child to understand the emotionally challenging event. Saying things like "That must have been so scary for you" or "I bet you were really afraid when that happened" can help a child put words to the emotions she may have felt during the event and acknowledges that you understand that her feelings are very powerful. Guiding the play to focus on solutions can be a useful way to help the child process the situation and understand that she is now safe.

Show and tell, or sharing time, can be especially challenging for children with incarcerated parents. When children are asked to share about themselves or their families, things can quickly become difficult for children of incarcerated parents and for you as a provider. Imagine the following scenario:

TEACHER: Okay, Rosa, it's your turn to share. What does
your mommy do?

ROSA (*quietly*): My mommy gone away.

TEACHER: Oh, where is she?

ROSA: She's in the big house.

BOBBY: What's the big house?

JAYDEN: My daddy says the big house is the place where
all the bad people go. Your mommy must be bad.

TEACHER (*trying to regain control and redirect conversation
to avoid the growing awkwardness of the situation*):
I'm sorry, Rosa. Okay, let's move on to Tracy. What
does your mommy do?

In situations like this, it is important to take the issue head-on in a non-judgmental, matter-of-fact manner. This is a learning opportunity for children. Though we often shy away from exposing children to traditionally negative subjects like prison and jail, shying away may actually create more stigma around Rosa and her mother than discussing the topic more openly. The following is the same scenario with a more open dialogue about Rosa's mother:

TEACHER: Okay, Rosa, it's your turn to share. What does
your mommy do?

ROSA (*quietly*): My mommy gone away.

TEACHER: Oh, where is she?

ROSA: She's in the big house.

BOBBY: What's the big house?

JAYDEN: My daddy says the big house is the place where
all the bad people go. Your mommy must be bad.

TEACHER: Bobby, the big house is what we sometimes
call "jail." Sometimes people make mistakes and break
the rule, or law. When they break a law, sometimes
they have to go to jail. Jayden, Rosa's mom isn't a bad
person, she just made a mistake.

BOBBY: What do mommies and daddies do when they're
in jail?

TEACHER: Well, sometimes they learn or play or do
  chores, just like you do.

JAYDEN: Do mommies and daddies stay a long time?

TEACHER: Sometimes, but sometimes they come home
  after just a little while. But while they're gone, they
  miss their families very much.

ROSA: I miss my mommy a lot.

TEACHER: I know you're sad, Rosa. We all feel sad sometimes when the people we love go away. But your
  mommy still loves you very much.

JAYDEN (*puts an arm around Rosa to hug her*): I miss my
  mommy when she goes away too.

This type of open dialogue spurred more questions from the inquisitive children in the room while also acknowledging Rosa's feelings and experiences. By the end, Jayden progressed from thinking about Rosa as having a "bad mom" to being sad that Rosa's mom has gone away. This type of conversation is not always easy to lead, however. It is difficult to anticipate what other children in the room may have heard about incarceration, so sometimes you may have to do some reframing of the conversation to get it to an open and honest place, lacking in judgment.

LIFE WITHOUT A HOME: YOUNG CHILDREN AND HOMELESSNESS

Homelessness is a different kind of loss that children can experience. Estimates indicate that 23 percent of all homeless people in 2013 were under the age of eighteen. Fifty-eight percent of all homeless people within families were under eighteen years of age (US Department of Housing and Urban Development Office of Community Planning and Development 2013). These staggering figures highlight the prevalence of children experiencing early life without a place to call home. Generally, families who are homeless are composed of single women and their children—the presence of a male figure in the family is fairly uncommon. Children in these families tend to be young children (birth to age five) or early school-age children (under age ten). Additionally, most homeless families seek refuge in homeless shelters or from friends or family, as opposed to living on the streets (Haber and Toro 2004).

Research

Homeless families are faced with a series of challenges, including decisions about where to seek shelter. Often mothers will ask friends or family to take in their children instead of facing shelter or street life as a family (Haber and Toro 2004). Mothers may then live on the streets or seek help from adult-only shelters. This choice leads to a separation of children from their caregivers for an unknown amount of time. This is stressful not only for the mother but also for the children (David, Gelberg, and Suchman 2012). As highlighted in the previous chapter, it is difficult for very young children to maintain attachment relationships with caregivers with whom they do not have contact on a regular basis. Though children may be staying with friends or family, a separation from the mother for an extended period can be disruptive to children's sense of security and safety. Very young children may struggle to understand their mother's decision to leave them with alternate caregivers (David, Gelberg, and Suchman 2012). They feel a great sense of grief and loss at the parent's departure. This stressful separation only adds to the stress already placed on young children who are facing a new, potentially unsafe environment. Without their parent and primary attachment figures to help them deal with the stress, they may begin to exhibit emotional and behavior challenges.

In cases where the mother does stay with her children, there are likely to be other challenges. When seeking assistance and support, much of a person's day is spent waiting in lines and meeting with social service providers. These can be very stressful encounters, adding to an already heavy burden. Furthermore, many social service waiting areas are not child-friendly spaces. As a result, children may become bored and act out during these long days, which can put additional strain on the already stressed mother. Feelings of inadequacy as a parent, failure to provide for her children, and emotional strain throughout the struggle of getting back on her feet may become overwhelming. In addition, parents may struggle with other challenges, such as mental and physical health issues, substance abuse, and extreme poverty

(David, Gelberg, and Suchman 2012). These risk factors can further increase the challenge of providing much-needed responsive care for children.

Mothers who are homeless also tend to be poorly educated, be unemployed, and may lack necessary skills for future employment (David, Gelberg, and Suchman 2012). Additionally, children from homeless families are more likely to be exposed to family and neighborhood violence, abuse, poverty, and hunger (Haber and Toro 2004). It is difficult to discuss homelessness without also discussing economic disadvantage. Substance use, domestic violence, neighborhood crime, and mental and physical illnesses are all common risk factors in the case of poverty and homelessness. However, some research suggests that homelessness may contribute unique challenges in the form of poor health and educational outcomes for children (Masten 2014).

More recent research on resilience in homeless families suggests that quality of parenting plays a major role in promoting positive outcomes for children. For children who face greater adversity, the positive, quality relationship with a caregiver provides a buffering effect, increasing the likelihood that children are more able to cope with the stress of homelessness. Quality parenting was found to be especially important for promoting academic success (Herbers 2011). Because of the serve-and-return relationship between children and their caregivers, it is also likely that the caregivers' ability to cope in the face of stress is a crucial factor in resilience for their children (Masten 2014).

Conversely, children may be a source of added stress to the situation through a trying relationship with their caregivers. Children's attempts to engage with the mother may be perceived as burdensome and difficult to manage (David, Gelberg, and Suchman 2012). The mother's stress coupled with her children's stress builds on itself, layer upon layer. Despite a parent's best efforts, the stress of the situation may make a parent less able to be responsive and comforting with her young children. Young children may perceive and internalize the parent's stress and, consequently, become confused or feel helpless (Haber and Toro 2004). Just as with children experiencing the trauma of maltreatment, homeless children experiencing extreme stress may exhibit subsequent challenging behaviors as an effort to seek safety and security in a chaotic or threatening environment.

Children who are homeless lack a secure sense of place. With the constant transitions between temporary shelters, or between friends' or family homes, children's typical patterns are interrupted. Homeless families often report many moves prior to, during, and following the period of homelessness (Haber and Toro 2004). For older children who can understand an explanation of why they are transitioning so frequently, this may be less of a challenge. However, to very young children who have limited language skills to understand the circumstances, and who are still learning the basic patterns of everyday life, these transitions can be very disruptive and stressful (Haber and Toro 2004).

Response

As with children who experience other types of trauma, homeless children may show behavioral regression (exhibiting behaviors typical of children younger than their chronological age), have difficulty sitting still, and may be hypervigilant (Koplow 2007). As discussed in chapter 5, hypervigilance is being constantly on the lookout for perceived threats. Building a close relationship with these children may be especially beneficial to help them feel comfortable in the care environment. Transitions between activities in the classroom may be especially challenging, so making yourself or another teacher available to assure children of their security in the midst of transition can be very helpful (Koplow 2007).

Children who are homeless also often struggle with self-regulation and executive functions. *Self-regulation* refers to the ability to control your behaviors. *Executive function* (EF), a related concept, refers to the ability to engage in a planned, goal-directed action. EF encompasses a number of skills, including inhibitory control (the ability to withhold a practiced response), working memory (the ability to keep information in mind and manipulate it), planning (the ability to think ahead about the required actions), and flexible task switching (switching back and forth between different rules) (Zelazo, Carlson, and Kesek 2008). Children who struggle with EF often have difficulty in early care environments because they are likely to act out, have limited control of their behaviors, and struggle with playing well with peers. EF and self-regulation difficulties are fairly common in children experiencing trauma.

Specifically in homeless children, EF has been found to be an important factor in promoting resilience. In older homeless children, strong EF abilities predict better academic performance measures (Masten 2014; Obradović 2009). As EF involves skills such as self-control, planning behaviors, and understanding rules, it is not surprising that EF abilities are very beneficial for children experiencing homelessness. Furthermore, quality parenting (for example, reading and talking with children, modeling problem-solving skills, providing emotional support) influences the development of EF. For children facing the stress of homelessness, quality parenting strengthens EF skills, which in turn bolster academic success (Herbers et al. 2011). Indeed, EF skills are important for all young children, but it appears that EF abilities are especially useful in helping children cope and thrive in the context of homelessness (Masten 2014).

Quality caregiver relationships are not the only thing that can increase EF abilities in young children. In fact, research has recently demonstrated that self-regulation and EF can be trained, like a muscle (Diamond and Lee 2011). Activities and games that can be used in the classroom to help strengthen EF include Simon Says; Red Light, Green Light; computer games; aerobics; martial arts; and yoga (Diamond and Lee 2011). Additionally, teachers can help children practice their EF skills throughout the day during simple tasks. For example, if you are asking children to line up to go outside and play, you might say, "Okay, it's time to line up for recess!" and expect all children to know and be able to complete the steps necessary for going out for recess. In reality, going to recess may require multiple steps. Children may need to (1) put away their current activities, (2) go to their cubbies, (3) pick up their coats, (4) put on their coats, (5) go to the wall to line up, (6) remember who they are supposed to stand next to, and (7) stand still and wait for the next instruction. What seems to us to be a simple command of "lining up for recess" can turn into a multistep sequence wherein children must keep all the steps in mind in the correct sequence.

However, children who struggle with executive functions may have difficulty completing the task, not because they don't want to, but because they don't have the skills to complete the different steps without additional help. Children who have EF difficulties may get easily distracted, forget the steps, or complete the steps out of order (lining up before getting their coats). Some children may require guidance in the form of breaking down the sequence into smaller steps. For example, you might say, "Okay, Sam, go over to your cubby, pick up your coat, and come back to me." Once Sam returns with the coat, you might say, "Here, I'll help you put on your coat." Then, reminding the child of the next step in the sequence, you could say, "Okay, now I want you to stand along the wall. Do you remember who you stand next to?" Lastly, you could remind Sam of the rules for waiting in line for recess by saying, "Good job! Remember to stand quietly and keep your hands to yourself." Regularly reminding children of rules and encouraging them to help remind others may also help children remember to control their behaviors (Koplow 2007). You might say, "Remember, during circle time we keep our hands to ourselves. Can you help remind each other?" For children experiencing homelessness, these regular reminders can be beneficial during a time when the rest of their lives are chaotic and lack structure.

It should be noted that not all children will require this level of a step-by-step reminder of the sequence and rules. However, if children seem unable to control themselves during these types of transitions or tasks, it is worth providing a breakdown of the steps to help children organize their behaviors. You may find after a few weeks of doing this that children are easily able to complete the sequence without your assistance. Others may need additional help for longer periods of time. It is important to be responsive to the individual child's needs in these cases.

Another way to help build self-control and EF in children is by giving them opportunities to make choices within a structure. This allows them to become active creators of their own learning. Giving children choices doesn't have to mean letting them choose from all the available options. For example, whenever I walk down the cereal aisle in the grocery store, I'm paralyzed with having too many choices. The abundance of options is overwhelming, and I suddenly have a complete inability to make any decisions. Giving children choices doesn't have to be this way. In fact, providing two or three discrete options can be a successful way to allow for some autonomy while still maintaining a structure. Providing situations where children can make choices may lower the chances of children acting out inappropriately (Kaiser and Rasminsky 2012). For example, you might ask the class at the beginning of the day, "Should we write the word *hello* or the words *good morning* on the board today?" Children can then indicate which choice they would prefer. Choosing *hello* or *good morning* doesn't change the way the day will progress, nor does it alter your original plan to have the children work on sounding out the letters of a word one by one. However, it does give children some choice in their learning. It allows them to become active creators.

One provider I interviewed for this book expressed the need for flexibility within early childhood curricula. One year her class got to do a dinosaur unit. This followed a unit about building. The children, who were excited about having just learned all about how to build exciting things (like catapults) said they wanted to build a catapult for the dinosaur figures they were learning about in the dinosaur unit. So they spent the majority of the two weeks building a dinosaur catapult so that they could make the dinosaurs fly up and hit the ceiling. Instead of immediately rejecting the idea in favor of sticking to the curriculum of memorizing the names of all the dinosaurs, this

OTHER WAYS YOU CAN PROVIDE STRUCTURED AUTONOMY

1. **To resolve sharing conflicts:** "Matthew, David wants to play with the fire truck next. Would you like to play with the fire truck for two or three more minutes?"

2. **To select art supplies:** "Would you like the crayons or the finger-paints today?"

3. **To arrange play themes:** "Do you want to play dolls with Cindy or play house with José?"

4. **To choose a snack:** "Would you like apples or carrots for your snack?"

5. **To initiate behavior modification:** "I can see you need help sitting still. Would you like to sit with me or Ms. Karly?"

Because there are so many cases where rules and structure are needed to help organize children's behavior, having daily situations in which children can have the freedom to choose what they would like to do from a few options gives them the sense that they have choices in their own learning.

care provider helped the children safely create a dinosaur catapult. It took a few days of intensive problem solving and trial and error, but eventually the children worked together to create a catapult that launched the dinosaurs into the air, a few soaring high enough to hit the ceiling. The children had a lot of fun building the catapult. With the teacher's guidance, they learned how to cooperate, problem solve, and create something new that had never been created before. As a result, the children excitedly talked about that dinosaur catapult for the rest of the year (S. Bellows, personal communication, March 2014). Instead of resorting to following the instructions of the curriculum, this teacher followed the lead of the students, allowing them to be active creators of their own learning. She maintained the rules of classroom safety and provided guidance and input while also allowing children a certain degree of autonomy in the process of their learning. Though the children did not learn the names of every dinosaur in the curriculum unit, they were instilled with an interest in the learning process and had an opportunity to practice many of the skills that are important for later academic success like problem solving, cooperation, and self-control.

CONCLUSIONS

Children may experience a variety of types of loss throughout early childhood. Loss of a home, the absence of a parent, or the death of a caregiver can be significant traumas. With the loss or estrangement of a primary caregiver, young children may find it especially difficult to understand and accept these losses. They may become emotional and more frequently act out. Providing consistent structure and messages in the child care environment can be especially beneficial for children experiencing such losses. Though it may feel harsh or even counterproductive, being open and honest with young children may help them understand and begin to process their emotions. The resources found on my website (www.drlangworthy.com) provide more direct guidance in dealing with children who are experiencing various forms of loss.

LINGERING QUESTIONS

➤ **A child in my care talks about her dead father as if he is alive. What do I do?** Be sure to consult with the family, if at all possible, to ensure that you are being respectful of any private wishes they may have on the matter. However, it is generally better to be straightforward with young children and remind them of the reality of the parent's death rather than carry on an illusion (say, "Your daddy is dead, and that's really sad," instead of, "Your daddy has gone away for a long time"). Though it may seem heartless in the short term, it may help the child better recover from the loss.

➤ **A mother of a child in my care says she hasn't told her son about his father being in prison and has instead told him that he's gone away to college. Should I maintain this story?** This is difficult. In general, it's important to respect the family's wishes on the matter. Remaining focused on the fact that "Daddy misses you very much while he's gone" still validates the child's feelings about missing the lost parent without getting into where the father is.

➤ **What kinds of games and activities can I do with children to help build self-regulation and executive function?** Simon Says and Red Light, Green Light are favorite games to play that work to strengthen executive function and self-regulation. Consider any game or activity that requires children to practice following rules or stopping a practice action (when the music plays, you jump up and down; when it stops, you freeze), or where they have to plan out a sequence of steps to complete a task (creating a play plan that has various steps to make a paper dog with pipe cleaners, craft sticks, glue, and markers) can help children practice executive function and self-regulation skills.

7 Reenvisioning the Response: Where We Go from Here

Not everything that is faced can be changed, but nothing can be changed until it is faced.

JAMES BALDWIN

OWNING WHAT YOU BRING TO THE TABLE

Memory is a funny thing. Our memories are often triggered by the briefest whiff of a scent or the shortest line of a melody. The photo of a time long past or the rough contours of an old blanket can transport us to memories of long ago. Memory can elicit biological reactions and waves of strong emotions that may seem uncontrollable. Sometimes these reactions are because of pleasant, happy memories. Other times those reactions can hurtle us back into memories of our own trauma or loss. You have probably experienced situations where you have intense emotional reactions because a child's behavior triggered an emotional memory for you. These memories may cause your own emotions to bubble up to the point where you feel like you are losing control. You may experience very strong physiological responses related to those heightened feelings, such as increased heart rate, sweating, and heavy breathing. As we established in the first section of this book, humans learn from their environment, and learning is built into the structure and function of the brain. Just as children learn to react in the presence of threatening environments, we adults carry our experiences with us, and occasionally our responses to past threats are triggered in ways that we never anticipated. You have those reactions for a reason. Figuring out what those reasons are may require deep reflection and personal exploration.

The exploration of your own experiences and how they might be affecting the way you interact with those around you is a crucial step in the process to becoming more emotionally aware and responsive. If you find that your work with children who have experienced trauma brings up difficult memories or uncontrollable emotions, you may find helpful ways to explore this through writing or talking with a therapist or counselor. A trained counselor will know what questions to ask and how best to support your exploration of difficult memories and experiences. Just as a primary strategy for working with young children is giving them words to express their intense emotions, the same strategy is employed in counseling or therapy.

Secondary Trauma

Working with children who have experienced trauma and loss can be particularly difficult. Adults may experience very real psychological and physiological traumatic responses to working with these children day after day. This is called *secondary trauma* and is an occupational hazard for people who work in caring roles. With secondary trauma, you essentially take on and experience the child's stress. Physiologically, the body reacts very similarly to a PTSD response (NCTSN 2011). People experiencing secondary traumatic stress may feel guilty, fearful, hopeless, hypervigilant, tired, angry, or cynical.

Secondary trauma is fairly common in professionals who work with highly traumatized individuals. Secondary trauma is also related to high turnover rates in those who work with traumatized or high-risk populations (NCTSN 2011). Workers who experience secondary trauma are considerably less effective at providing quality care. Seeking help and support with these experiences of secondary trauma is critical, as they can be detrimental for psychological as well as physical health and well-being. Getting support from supervisors and colleagues within your organization is especially important if you are struggling with secondary trauma. Furthermore, learning more about the potential triggers of secondary trauma as well as strategies for handling the highly emotional nature of working with traumatized children can be helpful in minimizing the experiences of secondary trauma (NCTSN 2011).

Exploring Your Triggers

Here are some simple steps you can take on your own to better understand how your experiences may influence your day-to-day reactions:

1. Write a list of the things in your work with children that you find most frustrating.

2. Record how your body responds when children do those things that you find the most frustrating. Does your heart pound? Do you feel out of breath? Do your palms become sweaty?

3. Think about the experiences with children you find especially frustrating and reflect on why these episodes might contribute to particularly strong emotional responses. Is a child's behavior triggering something in you? Is it a difficult experience you've had? Is it a painful memory?

4. List a few potential coping strategies you can use "in the moment" to help manage your emotions. Take a deep breath, count to ten, switch out with another provider, step into another room, and so on.

5. Write down more long-term self-care strategies. Take a long walk after work, talk with a friend or colleague, practice yoga, go to a movie, enjoy an evening out with your family, and so on.

6. Keep this list of care strategies somewhere you will see it often. Awareness of trigger behaviors will help keep you one step ahead of unintended emotional reactions.

It can also be beneficial to talk with other care providers about their experiences to learn how they handle such triggers. It may also be useful to attend trainings or workshops, or read more about what types of strategies you can employ to address your reactions to stress. My website (www.drlangworthy.com) has more information on these types of resources.

Reflective Practice

Reflective practice has been a standard method used in many areas of education since the 1930s (Gatti, Watson, and Siegel 2011). It has many definitions across different professions; however, the focus of reflective practice in the context of education is to use a problem-solving process to examine behaviors and responses to behaviors (Finlay 2008; Gatti, Watson, and Siegel 2011). Essentially, reflective practice involves gaining new insights by reflecting on previous experience.

Reflective practice requires stepping back from the emotional responses triggered by behaviors or experiences and seeking to understand, learn, and grow from those experiences. This is often an interactive process where professionals share ideas and learning openly with one another. In its more traditional form, the focus of reflective practice is on gathering data from observing and reflecting on responses to children's behaviors and working toward a better understanding of how professionals can more effectively address those behaviors.

More recently, reflective practice has evolved to address the complexities of working with stressed and traumatized children and their families. In these contexts, reflective practice is intended to address the importance of the various relationships in children's lives (parent-child, child-child, teacher-child, teacher-parent). Family contexts and relationships also become major points of discussion (Gatti, Watson, and Siegel 2011). The complexities of children's relationships are considered as major catalysts for challenging behaviors as well as potential areas of intervention.

Reflective practice takes place in the context of relationships and is not an isolated process. Working with a skilled facilitator and with other colleagues may be especially beneficial to most effectively reflect on the professional's emotional responses to children's behaviors and also the potential approaches to addressing those behaviors. When a facilitator uses open-ended, nonjudgmental questions ("How are things going with you?" or "What do you think that behavior might be about?") it establishes a safe space for professionals to openly share their thoughts and feelings, and tends to elicit the most productive responses (Gatti, Watson, and Siegel 2011).

Several challenges exist when engaging in reflective practice, including the large amount of time it requires, as well as how much administrators and organizational leaders value this practice (Finlay 2008). Additionally, some professionals may not want to participate in reflective practice so as to avoid feeling vulnerable about their struggles in front of peers and superiors. However, everyone can learn from reflective practice. Though it may be especially important for less experienced providers, even skilled providers can benefit from the practice. Reflective practice may be one way to encourage veteran teachers to break old habits and integrate new information about what is most effective for teaching young children (Kremenitzer 2005).

Reflective practice is just one potential option for maintaining self-care and addressing issues of secondary trauma. It is recognized as an effective approach (if conducted appropriately) to lessen your stress, help you feel more confident and supported, assist you to integrate new teaching strategies, and increase your understanding about the children in your care. See my website for more on secondary trauma (www.drlangworthy.com), or consider seeking out available options for engaging in reflective practice in your own community.

WORKING WITH FAMILIES

It can be difficult to keep from feeling overwhelmed or powerless when working with children who are dealing with trauma and loss. Throughout this book, a heavy emphasis has been placed on the importance of building strong relationships with children to promote resilience. But when working to build those relationships with children, it is important to be aware of other

contextual influences on young children, such as families, neighborhoods, and cultural communities. As a care provider, you may be in the position to develop relationships with children and also influence the other contexts that surround them every day. You may find there are ways to fluidly integrate different perspectives into your practice or to help support changes that promote children's resilience in families, neighborhoods, and communities.

Start by asking yourself, "What are the things that I can do in my practice to enhance the environments in which these children live?" Maybe you know children in your class whose parents would find parent education opportunities useful. Maybe you know children from families who have just moved and could use help accessing local resources in the community. Maybe there are opportunities to team up with other people or organizations in your neighborhood to provide more cohesive care for families experiencing trauma and loss.

As established previously, it is very useful to talk regularly with parents of children in your care. Parents' perspectives on their children's experiences can contribute to your ability to work with them. Talking with caregivers regularly also strengthens your relationship with them. However, in some cases, regular visits with parents may not be an option. Perhaps the children are bused into your care center or dropped off and picked up by a neighbor or family friend instead of a parent. In addition, parents may have histories of negative encounters with care providers or schools, which may limit your ability to engage with them. Some parents may be too stressed or disengaged to be available for your consultation. In these cases, it can be hard to build a relationship with the family, and consequently, it may prove to be challenging to understand the complex needs of the children.

To complicate matters, children and their parents may be experiencing the challenges of living in multiple cultures. Many children face the challenge of adapting flexibly to different cultural norms within the family and the care environment. Children and their parents may be dealing with the tension of experiencing new cultural traditions and practices while trying to maintain a connection to the home culture. In many cases, children and their parents are also tasked with learning a new language. Language can pose a significant barrier in the care environment for children. It can also be challenging for providers when they are working with parents who do not speak the language of the provider (Kaiser and Rasminsky 2012). It is common for children to serve as the interpreters between parents and providers, which raises concerns about what can and cannot be communicated through the child. This barrier may prevent parents from getting an accurate picture of what is happening in the care environment from providers and vice versa. When possible, it can be especially helpful to have translators or other people who can help bridge language and cultural barriers to increase understanding between care providers and families.

There are other ways that you may be able to encourage parents to feel welcome in the care environment. Some preschools provide a "parent room" for parents to spend time during the day (Koplow 2007). These parent rooms provide comfortable spaces where parents can meet with one another, care for their younger children, or just rest within the environment of the care center. These rooms are safe spaces for parents to spend time and may be a relief to parents who are especially stressed and concerned about their children's well-being. They may also learn effective parenting strategies from being in the context of the care environment (Koplow 2007).

In addition, providing opportunities for parent groups to meet regularly may be especially beneficial for families who are stressed and needing support from others in their communities. These groups may be educational in nature or may provide an open forum for parents to support one another. In neighborhoods experiencing high levels of violence, having a safe space for people to meet is an added draw. To keep it more informal, you might have a drop-in policy where parents can come in and meet with you or other staff as needed to discuss concerns about their children. Alternatively, you might consider contacting local organizations to be present to provide services and information, or have a therapeutic facilitator lead group discussions (Koplow 2007). Just as facilitated conversation can be beneficial for children's learning, as well as for reflection on your own practice, so, too, can this experience be helpful for parents in processing their own challenges and struggles. In the context of relationships with other parents, community leaders, therapeutic counselors, or supportive care providers, parents who are highly stressed may be able to find the safety and support they need to provide the best care for their children.

It should be noted that one of the biggest challenges in working with parents may be learning about some of their specific parenting practices. It may be easy to jump to the conclusion that a person is "a bad parent" or to think, "I can't believe they did that." However, care providers working with parents need to remember that, in most cases, parents are doing the best that they can with the resources they have available to them. It's as if you were a freshman in high school and expected to ace a college-level calculus class without having first taken algebra. You don't have the knowledge, skills, or capacity to ace the course. Instead, you're set up to fail from the start. This is how it can be for many parents who are experiencing toxic stress. They are doing the best they can with what they have, and yet they may regularly experience glares and judgment from other parents or from providers.

In order for trust to be built and change to occur, a neutral, nonjudgmental attitude is essential. Just as the strategies outlined throughout this book underscore the benefits of accepting and acknowledging a child's feelings while working to change the behaviors, the same perspective can be taken with parents. It is imperative that parents do not feel minimized, marginalized, or judged when they share their experiences or past parenting decisions. Shame and guilt are the antithesis of the healing process. Parents may previously have had damaging relationships with their children because of their own stresses, experiences, or lack of knowledge. However, the point is to focus on ensuring that those damaging forces don't continue to substantially hinder children's health and development. Partnering with trained therapeutic counselors may be a necessary step in providing support for parents. Access to educational as well as social and emotional support is crucial for parents to be able to build skills and confidence in their own abilities as parents.

An additional challenge, especially for underresourced and highly stressed families, is that they may be working with multiple social service organizations. Despite best intentions, these organizations are not always able to work cohesively with one another to provide the most comprehensive system of care for families. As a result, families may receive disjointed services, or worse, interaction with service agencies may add to the existing stress experienced by these families (Gearity 2009). Indeed, in most areas of the United States, effective, coordinated care for families is the exception rather than the rule. Yet it is important not to lose hope. Building relationships and working together with other organizations and service providers is essential to provide the most holistic care for families possible.

ORGANIZATIONAL PRACTICES: SEEKING SUPPORT

Often administrative and organizational policies that govern early care environments create more barriers than supports for professionals working with young children. Organizational principles must be supportive of care providers and recognize the diverse needs of staff and children in order to provide the highest-quality services. In cases where there is lack of administrative support, confusion, frustration, and burnout are more likely to occur. Furthermore, individuals who are stressed and feel unsupported by their employers tend to be less effective care providers and may inadvertently add more stress to already stressed children (Hodas 2006). Commitment from administrative staff is imperative in instituting principles of trauma-informed care. This administrative buy-in includes addressing changes not only in practices used in the care environment but also to the larger culture of the care community. This may include instituting a firm strengths-based focus, refraining from referring to children as "needy" or "deficient" and maintaining a soothing environment for children.

Not only is administrative buy-in of trauma-sensitive practices important, but it is also valuable for administrators and leaders to recognize the needs of care providers and provide opportunities for them to receive support. This may be in the form of reflective practice, as discussed previously. In addition, providing supportive staff meetings to discuss and resolve conflicts or barriers to learning may be beneficial. Allowing and encouraging providers to engage regularly with one another in learning different strategies can be an effective way of giving providers an opportunity to advance their skills. Providing support for professional development is also important. Furthermore, leaders need to vocally recognize providers' skills and acknowledge the hard work and expertise of those providers (Koplow 2007).

One practice that is becoming more common is more intentional supervision of care providers, especially those who are newer to the field. Usually supervision involves an experienced supervisor who observes a provider and then provides constructive feedback. This supervisor may also serve as a sounding board and confidant when difficulties arise. For this to be especially effective, the supervision needs to be consistent and engaged. Often in the world of education, supervision can mean a one-time visit to a classroom to gauge teaching skills and curriculum usage. For supportive supervision to be effective, more regular and consistent observations and meetings are required. In addition, just as children require a safe space to learn and grow, so do providers. It is imperative that care providers feel safe in expressing their feelings in reflection sessions (Koplow 2007). This supervision and reflection process provides newer teachers with an opportunity to think about their own practice and to hear experienced teachers' perspectives on challenging situations that arise in the care environment.

If you are reading this as a provider who does not have a supportive administrator, or you work in a smaller center or have your own family care service, you may wonder what options you have in order to find support. Reaching out to other providers you know may be an effective way to learn different strategies and tools. Engaging with other types of educators in your community may be beneficial. Even if these educators are focused on children of other age groups, just interacting with others who understand the challenges of working for many hours a day with children who experience trauma may be helpful. In addition, seeking out resources online or joining larger organizations or associations whose missions are to support child care providers may be especially helpful ways to broaden your networks and get exposed to more learning opportunities.

Partnering with Other Organizations

Obviously some of the biggest challenges to doing this type of supportive and reflective work are time and money. Though these are not small barriers and their influence on staff and administrators cannot be minimized, there may be some creative solutions to more effectively meet the needs of the organization. Most service providers across professions feel the tension of not having enough time. The caseloads are too large, there are too many children needing attention, too many patients, or too many families. This is an unfortunate reality that many providers face today. Though you cannot add hours to a day, you may be able to think about ways to use those hours more creatively and efficiently. What things that happen in your day must stay? What could go? Are there ways to employ the help of others to free up your own time? Getting creative about how you use your time may be an effective way to combat the stress of limited time.

The issue of money is a large barrier for many organizations that serve children and families. It's an unfortunate situation born out of more need than our systems are able to handle. However, as with thinking creatively about ways to use and reorganize your time, there may be ways to leverage strengths and resources of other people and organizations within your community to increase your own capacity. For example, my organization at the University of Minnesota has been partnering with a local elementary school to assist with creating trauma-sensitive environments in the school. Following a series of conversations about existing organizations that might be able to help, we connected with a local outpatient mental health services organization. As a result of that connection, the mental health organization is now providing mental health services on-site at the school for over fifty children and their families who were not previously receiving services. All of that started with a cup of coffee, shared interests, and a willingness to partner.

Through exploratory conversations, you may also discover local community resources and organizations that are available to you or the families you serve. These organizations may be able to provide additional services and supports for families in need. Searching the Internet is also a good way to find services and organizations in your area. Making connections with people in those organizations through informational interviews can be a useful way of gathering information and raising awareness for your own professional needs. On the whole, people who are working in professions in child and family services care deeply about the well-being of children. These professionals are likely trying to find ways to improve the lives of children in any way they can. Having conversations about concerns you have about the children in your care and asking for help in handling those issues may be the first step toward improving the ways children and families in your community are served.

It never hurts to inquire about the possibility of collaboration, receiving support, or increased partnership. Coordinating with parents on behavioral modification approaches to address children's disruptive behaviors both at home and in the early care environment can have better results than intervening in one environment alone. The same is true of larger organizational systems. Partnerships and coordination can increase reach, productivity, and the potential for greater change. Seeking out those other organizations, community supports, foundations, funders, or just other people in the community who care about the issue can open doors and lay the groundwork for currently unimaginable opportunities. Get creative about the barriers you face in your work. You may find there are more opportunities there than you thought.

MAKING PROGRESS

If you are unable to interact with many colleagues on a regular basis, you may feel somewhat isolated. Often, despite your efforts to improve the lives of the children you serve, you may find it especially frustrating when it feels like no one else in these children's lives seems to care about or understand their needs. Your efforts may seem hopeless given the pileup of adverse experiences and environments many of these children face on a daily basis. However, the issue of trauma is one of great concern to many people across the world. Trauma is becoming more well understood, its severity appreciated, and its treatment faced head-on.

Trauma's Context

Just as children have a variety of contexts that impact their development, trauma also occurs in, and is affected by, diverse contexts. As discussed earlier, there are many different experiences that constitute a "traumatic experience," but it is the individual's reaction to the event that determines whether that person experiences traumatic symptoms (Hodas 2006). Science indicates that a complex interplay of genetic and environmental experiences contribute to the severity of experienced traumatic stress, as well as to the risk factors for exposure to trauma (see chapter 4). For example, particularly complex factors such as a family history of mental illness and economic disparity contribute significantly to experiences of stress (Michaels, Borsheim, and Lohrbach 2010). In turn, each of these problems has many contributing factors, branching from individual and family-level challenges to broad-sweeping societal and policy issues. In other words, there are no quick fixes when it comes to trauma. The sheer breadth of the contributing factors to experiencing trauma and the dispersion of potential areas for intervention to treat and prevent traumatic stress is staggering. It can quickly begin to feel like a hopeless problem.

But you are not alone. Practitioners, researchers, and policy makers across the world recognize the diverse contexts that contribute to trauma and are working to create more positive and supportive environments where traumatic stress is minimized and effectively treated. You as a care provider are an integral piece of the puzzle. But you are not the only piece. Remind yourself of the people at all the different levels of various systems working to create sustainable change. Whether it is the local town council, a regional organization, a state university, Congress, or the United Nations, people at every level of our society are passionate about bettering the lives of children and families.

Through the coordination of these efforts, real and lasting change can occur. Though our current systems are not always set up to provide the most effective care and prevention of trauma, there are ways that you as a care provider can work to connect with other social service providers to coordinate care for the children and families you work with every day. Reaching out, making connections, building relationships—just like you do with the young children in your care every day—is a crucial part of the process of coordinating care.

Valuing Your Expertise

As you read this, you may feel like you don't have the required knowledge or expertise to create change on a larger scale than in your care environment. However, you bring a wealth of expertise that is crucial to the improvement of care for young children. You work with these children every day. You know what their needs are and what they crave. You know what will and won't work in a very real way. You may have been burned by the system before, and you've learned what supports you need to provide the best care possible.

Valuing that knowledge within yourself and learning to speak boldly about your experiences are the first steps to further integrating your knowledge into the broader conversation about change.

Maybe as you read this you're barely keeping your head above water. You feel overwhelmed with the sheer number of things you already have to do each day. Maybe you feel that you can't possibly take on anything else. If that is what you are feeling, you first need to take care of yourself. Burnout is a fairly common thing for professionals working with high-risk populations (NCTSN 2011). Everyone feels overwhelmed or ineffective at times. These are normal feelings but ones that should not be ignored. Focusing on self-care is the first step to feeling capable of creating a larger impact.

For those of you reading this and itching to do more, start to employ some of the strategies highlighted in the book. In addition to connecting with organizations and other professionals, and seeking out more opportunities for learning, you may be interested in getting involved in political change. Often the political system seems like more of a barrier than a support, but you as an individual hold power with those who represent you.

Over the last couple of years, I've been working a bit more in the policy arena. If I've learned anything, it is that constituents hold the power. If I, as someone from the university, show up for an appointment with a state representative, and a walk-in constituent shows up at the same time, in most cases the constituent will get to meet with the representative before I do. I've found that representatives and senators would much rather hear from their constituents, the people they are called to represent, than others in the community. It is their constituents they care about the most. You can use that power to your advantage and leverage your connections to educate your representatives and speak out for changes to policies that affect children and families.

As adults, we tend to think of our development as being complete and finished. However, development is an ongoing process across the life span. The journey of learning and discovery of your talents, skills, and abilities is ongoing. As you allow yourself the opportunity to explore those passions, you may find your talents used in ways you never previously considered. It is in that self-reflection and progress that learning and development occur. It is through building strong relationships and connections with others that we begin to bridge the gaps that exist in the ways we serve children and families. It is in that community of relationships that we all move forward together. When we all begin to share our experiences and bring the challenges we face to the attention of people working in other sectors and professions, eventually change can begin to happen. It's not a short or easy process, but it is possible and necessary.

CONCLUSIONS

If you've made it this far in the book, you've probably recognized that working with children who experience stress and trauma is a complex issue with no easy silver-bullet solutions. You may feel like you as an individual don't have much power. You may feel like this chapter on creating change just raises the bar on the expectations of you as a care provider. Maybe you wonder whether your efforts will make a bit of difference in the grand scheme of things. However, the more we all begin to understand the importance of promoting health and resilience in families and children as a complex issue, where everyone has a role to play, the more likely it is that things will change for the better for young children.

Throughout this book, I've tried to provide not only a description of the ways different experiences that young children have affect their development but also some practical ideas for how to help children build coping skills and resilience to trauma. There are many different factors and strategies to consider when working with children who have faced trauma, but if I could have you take away three messages from this book, they would be these:

- **Context is everything.** What surrounds us changes us. We are the complex interplay of our diverse experiences and our intricate biological systems. Human existence has never been, nor will it ever be, simple. But creating supportive contexts in which children can grow and learn will help build resilience to adversity.
- **We need to think complexly about our problems and about each other.** Trauma and adversity are not simple problems with simple solutions. Neither are our lives simple and straightforward. We must stop thinking about each other existing at only one end

of a spectrum. Instead, we must look at the complexities that we all face and understand that we are all trying to do the best we can with what we have.

- **Relationships matter.** Though you may never see how much, the relationships you build with young children will matter for years to come. The true power for healing lies in our human connections with one another. Our relationships with each other are what matter most.

Together, through our relationships with one another, we can re-envision our response to caring for children who experience trauma. When we travel the road together, leveraging our minds, skills, and relationships, we can bridge the gap and promote the best opportunities for young children.

LINGERING QUESTIONS

➤ **I'm feeling burned out trying to provide quality care to children who experience trauma and loss. What should I do?** Seek out your secure relationships. Find the people you care about and who care about you to get emotional support. Consider therapy or counseling to help you work through your feelings of being overwhelmed. You can also ask for help in your workplace if that's a possibility (for example, another employee, additional training, access to supervision, or reflective practice). In short, do the things you need to do to take care of yourself.

➤ **How do I get more support from my organization around trauma-informed care?** This is tough. Changing people's minds about procedures and how things operate can be challenging, but you might start by having a conversation with key decision makers about why trauma-informed care is important. Addressing how later academic success is connected to early childhood brain development and the effects of trauma on brain development may help make the link clearer. Though it can be difficult to provide trauma-informed care without administrative buy-in, you can still work to change the way you interact with the children in your care.

➤ **I want to contact my legislators about early childhood education. Where do I start?** Great! Find out who your local, state, and national representatives are. You can search the Internet for "Who is my state representative/senator?" and most state legislative websites have a place to put in your zip code to find out who your representatives and senators are. Then you can contact their offices to set up a meeting to talk more about your perspectives, or send a letter or e-mail telling them about your work with young children.

References

Ai, Amy L., Lovie J. Jackson Foster, Peter J. Pecora, Nancy Delaney, and Wenceslau Rodriguez. 2013. "Reshaping Child Welfare's Response to Trauma: Assessment, Evidence-Based Intervention, and New Research Perspectives." *Research on Social Work Practice,* 23(6): 651–68. doi:10.1177/1049731513491835.

Ainsworth, Mary D. Salter, Mary C. Blehar, Everett Waters, and Sally Wall. (1978) 2014. *Patterns of Attachment: A Psychological Study of the Strange Situation.* Reprint, Hove, East Sussex, UK: Psychology Press.

American Psychological Association. 2013n.d.. "Effects of Poverty, Hunger and Homelessness on Children and Youth." Retrieved April 06 from http://www.apa.org/pi/families/poverty.aspx?item=2.

Anne E. Casey Foundation. 2011. *Data Snapshot: On Foster Care Placement.* Baltimore, MD: The Annie E. Casey Foundation.

Bowlby, John. 1982. "Nature and Function of Attachment Behavior." In *Attachment and Loss,* vol. 1, 2nd ed., 210–34. New York: Basic Books.

Bronfenbrenner, Urie. 1979. *The Ecology of Human Development: Experiments by Nature and Design.* Boston: Harvard University Press.

Cicchetti, Dante. 2013. "Annual Research Review: Resilient Functioning in Maltreated Children—Past, Present, and Future Perspectives." *Journal of Child Psychology and Psychiatry* 54(4): 402–22. doi:10.1111/j.1469-7610.2012.02608.x.

Dallaire, Danielle H. and Laura C. Wilson. 2010. "The Relation of Exposure to Parental Criminal Activity, Arrest, and Sentencing to Children's Maladjustment." *Journal of Child and Family Studies* 19 (4): 404–418.

David, Daryn H., Lillian Gelberg, and Nancy E. Suchman. 2012. "Implications of Homelessness for Parenting Young Children: A Preliminary Review from a Developmental Attachment Perspective." *Infant Mental Health Journal* 33(1): 1–9. doi:10.1002/imhj20333.

De Young, Alexandra C., Justin A. Kenardy, and Vanessa E. Cobham. 2011. "Trauma in Early Childhood: A Neglected Population." *Clinical Child and Family Psychology Review* 14(3): 231–50. doi:10.1007/s10567-011-0094-3.

Diamond, Adele and Kathleen Lee. 2011. "Interventions Shown to Aid Executive Function Development in Children 4 to 12 Years Old." *Science* 333(959): 959–64. doi:10.1126/science.1204529.

Dowdney, Linda. 2000. "Annotation: Childhood Bereavement Following Parental Death." *Journal of Child Psychology and Psychiatry* 41(7): 819–30. doi:10.1111/1469-7610.00670.

Evans-Campbell, Teresa. 2008. "Historical Trauma in American Indian/Native Alaska Communities: A Multilevel Framework for Exploring Impacts on Individuals, Families, and Communities." *Journal of Interpersonal Violence* 23(3): 316–38. doi:10.1177/0886260507312290.

Felitti, Vincent J., Robert F. Anda, Dale Nordenberg, David F. Williamson, Alison M. Spitz, Valerie Edwards, Mary P. Koss, and James S. Marks. 1998. "Relationship of Childhood Abuse and Household Dysfunction to Many of the Leading Causes of Death in Adults: The Adverse Childhood Experiences (ACE) Study." *American Journal of Preventive Medicine* 14(4): 245–58.

Finlay, Linda. 2008. "Reflecting on 'Reflective Practice.'" Discussion paper prepared for Practice-Based Professional Learning Center.

Gatti, Shelley Neilson, Christopher L. Watson, and Carol F. Siegel. 2011. "Step Back and Consider: Learning from Reflective Practice in Infant Mental Health." *Young Exceptional Children* 14(2): 32–45. doi:10.1177/1096250611402290.

Gearity, Anne. 2009. *Developmental Repair: A Training Manual.* Minneapolis, MN: Washburn Center for Children.

Geoffroy, Marie-Claude, Sylvana M. Côté, Charles-Édouard Giguère, Ginette Dionne, Philip David Zelazo, Richard E. Tremblay, Michel Boivin, and Jean R. Séguin. 2010. "Closing the Gap in Academic Readiness and Achievement: The Role of Early Childcare." *Journal of Child Psychology and Psychiatry* 51(12): 1359–67. doi:10.1111/j.1469-7610.2010.02316.x.

Gewirtz, Abigail H., Christopher R. Erbes, Melissa A. Polusny, Marion S. Forgatch, and David S. Degarmo. 2011. "Helping Military Families through the Deployment Process: Strategies to Support Parenting." *Professional Psychology: Research and Practice* 42(1): 56–62. doi:10.1037/a0022345.

Gibson, Eleanor J., and Richard D. Walk. 1960. "The Visual Cliff." *Scientific American* 202(4): 64-71.

Gunnar, Megan R. 2001. "Effects of Early Deprivation: Findings from Orphanage-Reared Infants and Children." In *Handbook of Developmental Cognitive Neuroscience*, edited by C. A. Nelson and M. Luciana, 617–28. Cambridge, MA: MIT Press.

Haber, M. G. and P. A. Toro. 2004. "Homelessness among Families, Children, and Adolescents: An Ecological-Developmental Perspective." *Clinical Child and Family Psychology Review* 7(3): 123–64.

Harlow, Harry. 1958. "The Nature of Love." *American Psychologist* 13: 673–85.

Haskins, Ron and Cecelia Rouse. 2005. "Closing Achievement Gaps." Policy brief from The Future of Children. Princeton, NJ: Princeton University. Retrieved from http://futureofchildren.org/futureofchildren/publications/docs/15_01_PolicyBrief.pdf.

Herbers, Janette E., J. J. Cutuli, Theresa L. Lafavor, Danielle Vrieze, Cari Leibel, Jelena Obradović, and Ann S. Masten, 2011. "Direct and Indirect Effects of Parenting on the Academic Functioning of Young Homeless Children." *Early Education & Development* 22(1): 77–104. doi:10.1080/10409280903507261.

Hodas, G. R. 2006. *Responding to Childhood Trauma: The Promise and Practice of Trauma Informed Care*. National Association of State Mental Health Program Directors. Retrieved from http://www.nasmhpd.org/docs/publications/docs/2006/Responding%20to%20Childhood%20Trauma%20-%20Hodas.pdf.

Howes, Carollee. 2010. *Culture and Child Development in Early Childhood Programs: Practices for Quality Education and Care*. New York: Teachers College Press.

Howes, Carollee and Sharon Ritchie. 2002. *A Matter of Trust: Connecting Teachers and Learners in the Early Childhood Curriculum*. New York: Teachers College Press.

Hungerford, Anne, Sierra K. Wait, Alyssa M. Fritz, and Caroline M. Clements. 2012. "Exposure to Intimate Partner Violence and Children's Psychological Adjustment, Cognitive Functioning, and Social Competence: A Review." *Aggression and Violent Behavior* 17(4): 373–82. doi:10.1016/j.avb.2012.04.002.

Jacobson, Tamar. 2008. *Don't Get So Upset!* St. Paul, MN: Redleaf Press.

Jiang, Yang, Mercedes Ekono, and Curtis Skinner. 2014. "Basic Facts about Low-Income Children: Children under 3 Years, 2012." New York: National Center for Children in Poverty. Retrieved from http://www.nccp.org/publications/pdf/text_1087.pdf.

Kaiser, Barbara and Judy Sklar Rasminsky. 2012. *Challenging Behavior in Young Children: Understanding, Preventing and Responding Effectively*, 3rd ed. Boston: Pearson.

Koplow, Lesley, ed. 2007. *Unsmiling Faces: How Preschools Can Heal*, 2nd ed. New York: Teachers College Press.

Kremenitzer, Janet Pickard. 2005. "The Emotionally Intelligent Early Childhood Educator: Self-Reflective Journaling." *Early Childhood Education Journal* 33(1): 3–9. doi:10.1007/s10643-005-0014-6.

Lieberman, Alicia F., Ann Chu, Patricia Van Horn, and William W. Harris. 2011. "Trauma in Early Childhood: Empirical Evidence and Clinical Implications." *Development and Psychopathology* 23(02): 397–410. doi:10.1017/S0954579411000137.

Lieberman, Alicia F. and Patricia Van Horn. 2013. "Infants and Young Children in Military Families: A Conceptual Model for Intervention." *Clinical Child and Family Psychology Review* 16(3): 282–93. doi:10.1007/s10567-013-0140-4.

Main, Mary and Judith Solomon. 1990. "Procedures for Identifying Infants as Disorganized/Disoriented during the Ainsworthy Strange Situation." In *Attachment in the Preschool Years: Theory, Research, and Intervention*, edited by M. T. Greenburg, D. Cicchetti, and E. M. Cummings, 121–60. Chicago: University of Chicago Press.

Martin, T. Michael. 2013. *The End Games.* New York: Balzer & Bray.

Maruschak, Laura M., Lauren E. Glaze, and Christopher J. Mumola. 2010. "Incarcerated Parents and Their Children: Findings from the Bureau of Justice Statistics." In *Children of Incarcerated Parents: A Handbook for Researchers and Practitioners*, edited by J. Mark Eddy and Julie Poehlmann, 33–51. Washington DC: Urban Institute Press.

Masten, Ann S. 2014. *Ordinary Magic: Resilience in Development.* New York: The Guilford Press.

McAlister Groves, Betsy. 2013. "Addressing Early Childhood Trauma in the Context of the Child Welfare System." *CW 360°: A Comprehensive Look at a Prevalent Child Welfare Issue* Winter 2013: 20.

McDonald, Renee, Ernest N. Jouriles, Suhasini Ramisetty-Mikler, Raul Caetano, and Charles E. Green. 2006. "Estimating the Number of American Children Living in Partner-Violent Families." *Journal of Family Psychology* 20(1): 137–42. doi:10.1037/0893-3200.20.1.137.

Michaels, Cari, Christeen Borsheim, and Sue Lohrbach. 2010. "What Is Trauma and Why Is It Important?" *Children's Mental Health eReview* (May): 1–7.

Michaels, Cari, Rudy Rousseau, and Youa Yang. 2010. "Historical Trauma and Microaggressions: A Framework for Culturally-Based Practice." *Children's Mental Health eReview* (October): 1–9.

Miller, Peggy J., Karl S. Rosengren, and Isabel T. Gutierrez. 2014. "Introduction." *Monographs of the Society for Research in Child Development* 79(1): 1–18. doi:10.1097/HRP.0000000000000028.

National Opportunity to Learn Campaign. 2011. "Opportunity Gap." Cambridge, MA: National Opportunity to Learn Campaign. Retrieved from http://www.otlcampaign.org/sites/default/files/resources/Opportunity Gap Toolkit FINAL.pdf.

National Research Council and Institute of Medicine. 2000. *From Neurons to Neighborhoods: The Science of Early Childhood Development.* Washington D.C.: National Academy Press.

National Scientific Council on the Developing Child. 2004a. "Children's Emotional

Development Is Built into the Architecture of Their Brains: Working Paper No. 2." Cambridge, MA: Center on the Developing Child. Retrieved from http://www.developingchild.net.

———. 2004b. "Young Children Develop in an Environment of Relationships." Cambridge, MA: Center on the Developing Child. Retrieved from http://www.developingchild.net.

———. 2006. "Early Exposure to Toxic Substances Damages Brain Architecture: Working Paper No. 4." Cambridge, MA: Center on the Developing Child. Retrieved from http://www.developingchild.net.

———. 2007. "The Timing and Quality of Early Experiences Combine to Shape Brain Architecture: Working Paper No. 5." Cambridge, MA: Center on the Developing Child. Retrieved from http://www.developingchild.net.

———. 2009. "Maternal Depression Can Undermine the Development of Young Children: Working Paper No. 8." Cambridge, MA: Center on the Developing Child. Retrieved from http://www.developingchild.harvard.edu.

———. 2010. "Early Experiences Can Alter Gene Expression and Affect Long-Term Development: Working Paper No. 10." Cambridge, MA: Center on the Developing Child. Retrieved from http://www.developingchild.net.

———. 2012. "The Science of Neglect—The Persistent Absence of Responsive Care Disrupts the Developing Brain: Working Paper No. 12." Cambridge, MA: Center on the Developing Child. Retrieved from http://www.developingchild .harvard.edu.

———. 2014. "Excessive Stress Disrupts the Architecture of the Developing Brain: Working Paper No. 3." Cambridge, MA: Center on the Developing Child. Retrieved from http://www.developingchild.harvard.edu.

(NCTSN) National Child Traumatic Stress Network. n.d.-a. "Impact of Complex Trauma." Los Angeles, CA, and Durham, NC: NCTSN. Retrieved from http://www.nctsn.org/sites/default/files/assets/pdfs/impact_of_complex_ trauma_final.pdf.

———. n.d.-b. "Traumatic Grief in Military Children: Information for Educators." Los Angeles, CA, and Durham, NC: NCTSN. Retrieved from http://www .nctsn.org/sites/default/files/assets/pdfs/military_grief_educators.pdf.

———. 2004. "For School Personnel: Childhood Traumatic Grief Educational Materials." Los Angeles, CA, and Durham, NC: NCTSN. Retrieved from http://www.nctsn.org/sites/default/files/assets/pdfs/schools_package.pdf.

———. 2007. "Child Sexual Abuse Fact Sheet: For Parents, Teachers, and Other Caregivers." Los Angeles, CA, and Durham, NC: NCTSN. Retrieved from http://nctsn.org/sites/default/files/assets/pdfs/ ChildSexualAbuseFactSheetFINAL_10_2_07.pdf.

———. 2009. "Child Physical Abuse Fact Sheet: For Parents, Teachers, and Other Caregivers." Los Angeles, CA, and Durham, NC: NCTSN. Retrieved from http://nctsn.org/sites/default/files/assets/pdfs/ChildPhysicalAbuse_Factsheet.pdf.

———. 2011. "Secondary Traumatic Stress: A Fact Sheet for Child-Serving Professionals." Los Angeles, CA, and Durham, NC: NCTSN.

Obradović, Jelena. 2009. "Effortful Control and Adaptive Functioning of Homeless Children: Variable-Focused and Person-Focused Analyses." *Journal of Applied Developmental Psychology* 31(2): 109–17. doi:10.1016/j.appdev.2009.09.004.

Ogbu, John U. 1992. "Understanding Cultural Differences and School Learning." *Education Libraries* 16(3): 7–11.

Paris, Ruth, Ellen R. DeVoe, Abigail M. Ross, and Michelle L. Acker. 2010. "When a Parent Goes to War: Effects of Parental Deployment on Very Young Children and Implications for Intervention." *The American Journal of Orthopsychiatry* 80(4): 610–8. doi:10.1111/j.1939-0025.2010.01066.x.

Pathania, Manavendra and Angelique Bordey. 2013. "Postnatal Neurogenesis in the Subventricular Zone: A Manipulable Source for CNS Plasticity and Repair." In *Neural Stem Cells—New Perspectives*, edited by Luca Bonfanti, 137–61. doi:10.5772/55679.

Restak, R. 2001. *The Secret Life of the Brain*, 1st ed. Washington DC: Joseph Henry Press.

Sanchez, M. Mar and Seth D. Pollak. 2009. "Socioemotional Development Following Early Abuse and Neglect." In *Handbook of Developmental Social Neuroscience*, edited by Michelle De Haan and Megan R. Gunnar, 497–520. New York: Guilford Press.

Shlafer, Rebecca J., Erica Gerrity, Ebony Ruhland, and Marc Wheeler. 2013. "Children with Incarcerated Parents—Considering Children's Outcomes in the Context of Family Experiences." *Children's Mental Health eReview* (June): 1–17.

Shonkoff, Jack P. and Andrew S. Garner. 2012. "The Lifelong Effects of Early Childhood Adversity and Toxic Stress." *Pediatrics* 129(1): e232–46. doi:10.1542/peds.2011-2663.

Sorce, James, Robert Emde, Joseph J. Campos, and Mary D. Klinnert. 1985. "Maternal Emotional Signaling: Its Effect on the Visual Cliff Behavior of 1-Year-Olds." *Developmental Psychology* 21(1): 195–200. Retrieved from http://psycnet.apa.org/journals/dev/21/1/195/.

Spinazzola, Jonah, Mandy Habib, Angel Knoverek, Joshua Arvidson, Jan Nisenbaum, Robert Wentworth, Hilary Hodgdon, Andrew Pond, and Cassandra

Kisiel. 2013. "The Heart of the Matter: Complex Trauma in Child Welfare." *CW 360°: A Comprehensive Look at a Prevalent Child Welfare Issue* Winter 2013:8–9.

Stahl, Brandon. 2014. "Eric Dean: The Boy They Couldn't Save." *StarTribune.* Retrieved from http://www.startribune.com/local/273325741.html.

Sue, Derald Wing, Christina M. Capodilupo, Gina C. Torino, Jennifer M. Bucceri, Aisha M. B. Holder, Kevin L. Nadal, and Marta Esquilin. 2007. "Racial Micro-aggressions in Everyday Life: Implications for Clinical Practice." *The American Psychologist* 62(4): 271–86. doi:10.1037/0003-066X.62.4.271.

Tervalon, Melanie and Jann Murray-García. 1998. "Cultural Humility versus Cultural Competence: A Critical Distinction in Defining Physician Training Outcomes in Multicultural Education." *Journal of Health Care for the Poor and Underserved* 9(2): 117–25. doi:10.1353/hpu.2010.0233.

US Department of Housing and Urban Development, Office of Community Planning and Development. 2013. *The 2013 Annual Homeless Assessment Report (AHAR) to Congress.* Washington, DC.

US Census Bureau. 2012. "U.S. Census Bureau Projections Show a Slower Growing, Older, More Diverse Nation a Half Century from Now." Retrieved from https://www.census.gov/newsroom/releases/archives/population/cb12-243.html.

US Department of Health and Human Services, Administration for Children and Families. 2013. "Data Brief 2013-1 Recent Demographic Trends in Foster Care." Retrieved from http://www.acf.hhs.gov/programs/cb/resource/data-brief-trends-in-foster-care-1.

US Department of Health and Human Services; Administration for Children and Families; Administration on Children Youth and Families; and Children's Bureau. 2012. *Child Maltreatment 2012.* Retrieved from http://www.acf.hhs.gov/programs/cb/research-data-technology/statistics-research/child-maltreatment.

University of Pittsburgh Office of Child Development. n.d.. "Indiscriminate Friendliness." Retrieved from http://www.ocd.pitt.edu/Files/PDF/Foster/27758_ocd_Indiscriminate_Friendliness.pdf.

VanZomeren-Dohm, Adrienne, Rowena Ng, Kamyala Howard, Molly Kenney, Lynde Ritchmeier Cyr, and Jessica Gourneau. 2013. "How Trauma 'Gets Under the Skin': Biological and Cognitive Processes of Child Maltreatment." *Children's Health eReview* (March): 1–17.

Wilson, Charles, Lisa Conradi, Erika Tullberg, Erin Sullivan Sutton, and Christeen Borsheim. 2011. "Creating Trauma-Informed Systems of Child Welfare." *Children's Mental Health eReview* (March): 1–11.

Zeanah, Charles H., Carole Shauffer, and Mary Dozier. 2011. "Foster Care for Young Children: Why It Must Be Developmentally Informed." *Journal of the American Academy of Child and Adolescent Psychiatry* 50(12), 1199–1201. doi:10.1016/j.jaac.2011.08.001

Zelazo, Philip D., Stephanie M. Carlson, and Amanda Kesek. 2008. "The Development of Executive Function in Childhood." In *Handbook of Developmental Cognitive Neuroscience*, edited by C. A. Nelson and M. Luciana, 553–574. Cambridge, MA: MIT Press.

Index

physical, 93–94, 95
sexual, 94
rules in care environment about,
    108
as witnesses to domestic abuse
    caregiver's response to, 107–110

case example, 104–105
effects of, 104–106
"Visual Cliff" experiment, 18
voluntary minority groups, 57
Vygotsky, Lev, 20